MW01680953

THE SELF-AWARE INTERVIEW

JOB INTERVIEW ESSENTIALS FOR EVERY ENNEAGRAM TYPE

CAROLYN ILLMAN

Published by Hire Possibilities Press, Seattle, Washington
Human Authored Reg #: 4969167, https://authorsguild.org/human

For more information, email carolyn@hirepossibilitiesseattle.com

ISBN: 979-8-9952986-0-1 - Paperback
ISBN: 979-8-9952986-1-8 - eBook
ISBN: 979-8-9952986-2-5 - hardcover

DISCLAIMER

DEDICATION

I dedicate this book to anyone who needs to be reminded of the special and unique qualities they bring to every room they walk into. Never doubt yourself or forget who you are.

This book is also dedicated to my parents, Linda and Craig; my husband, Colin; my cousin, Jen; and my childhood friend Rose, who have always encouraged me to write.

Hazel – May you stay endlessly curious, connect with everyone you meet, know your strengths, and never feel you must be perfect to be whole.

LET'S CONNECT!

Follow Carolyn / Hire Possibilities on Instagram or subscribe to the newsletter for more ideas on interviewing well, hiring thoughtfully, and understanding the Enneagram.

Instagram: @hirepossibilities

Website: www.hirepossibilitiesseattle.com

CONTENTS

INTRODUCTION

YOU NEVER KNOW what you're walking into when you step into a job interview. When I think of my first one, I remember my stomach turning and the deafening tick of the clock on the wall. I remember the awkward pauses as I searched for my next response, wondering what impression I was leaving on the person across the table.

In the years since, the roles have been reversed. I've conducted hundreds of interviews, and each one reminds me how vulnerable the process feels and how much anxiety it can stir in even the most capable person.

For nearly two decades, I've had a front-row seat to interviews in conference rooms, over video calls, and in final rounds where futures are decided, as both a job seeker and an interviewer. I've seen what resonates, what creates doubt, and what helps someone walk out of the room with a confident yes.

I've helped candidates prepare, and I've helped companies decide. I've watched talented people underestimate themselves and solid teams make the wrong selection because they weren't clear on what they were truly looking for. When you spend years approaching these interviews and outcomes with curiosity, patterns begin to emerge. This book is my way of sharing those patterns with you.

What works isn't perfection or memorization. It's self-awareness. Success rarely comes from having the "perfect" answer. It comes from understanding who you are and communicating clearly so the person across the table can fully understand you. That's what we're going to work on together.

Authenticity and Vulnerability

My best interviews, both as a candidate and as an interviewer, were those where I felt fully comfortable being authentic and vulnerable. Knowing yourself is the essential first step to doing this consistently, and if you aren't sure what's holding you back or where to start, the Enneagram is a tool that can simplify the process (more on this later).

I first unlocked that authenticity and vulnerability when I was in my second in-person interview for a job at my dream company, around the time of the Great Recession of 2008. I was excited about this digital agency, one that would give me the opportunity to work on children's television content, with clients including the Disney Channel, PBS, and Nickelodeon. I just knew I would be a great fit at this organization— so much so that I had turned down a handful of full-time roles offered to me by other companies during the three-month interview process. I had very little professional experience at the time, only three internships under my belt, and it was an uphill battle to convince them to give me a chance in this role.

When I was back in the room for my second interview, I found myself staring at a panel of six interviewers, three of whom were at the most senior level of the company. I was nervous, but I was motivated by my certainty that I would excel at this position. Frankly, I was also a little annoyed at how long the process had taken.

"Have you looked at our website?" the executive art director asked me.

I took a moment and a deep breath before responding. Yes, as an Enneagram 6 with an extremely strong 5 wing (though I didn't know it at the time), I had spent hours exhaustively looking at their website during the interview process. Each time I looked at the website, I felt myself increasingly caught up in how much I wanted to work there. When I wasn't sure if I was going to be called back over the past couple of weeks, I had decided to take a break from ruminating over it.

Without fully thinking through my answer, I mused aloud, "You know when you break up with your boyfriend and you keep looking at his Facebook page because you wish you were still together, but you realize you have to stop since it's not good for you?"

Everyone in the room blinked; they seemed amused, concerned, and unsure where I was going with this.

"I've spent a lot of time looking at your website over the past couple of months, but I haven't looked recently because I've had these great interviews, followed by gaps of time where I don't hear back. I really want this job. I'm happy to answer any questions you have about your website based on the research I've previously done, but if any changes have been made in the past couple of weeks, I haven't seen them."

I give you full permission to cringe at 21-year-old me. I don't necessarily recommend pivoting your interviewer's question to talk about your own priorities, but that's what I did. My biggest concern was making sure they knew how serious I was about this role. In the process, I showed them I had a sense of humor and that I was human.

They loved the metaphor. They laughed, immediately apologized for not getting back to me quickly enough, and made sure the rest of the hiring process went smoothly. As I walked out the door, I apologized to my future manager for calling her out about leaving me hanging.

She immediately put me at ease: "Your persistence is exactly why we think you'd be a good fit for this role."

Another reason I felt comfortable sharing this answer with my interviewers was they did such a great job of making me feel at ease. They knew I was nervous, so they created a safe environment where I could share my experiences, and they could get to know me better. As an Enneagram 6, a type characterized by anxiety, I needed to feel psychologically safe to be able to share my true feelings.

To be clear, I'm not telling you to do exactly this in your next interview. This worked specifically for the person I was at 21; I was able to read the room and know how my words would land. I hadn't planned to say this. I also hadn't memorized any responses to common questions or rehearsed how I would answer them.

All too often, participants are looking for easy solutions to ace an interview with memorized responses. Interviewers try asking candidates the "best" questions. Candidates and companies continue to look for hacks to make the entire process easier, until everyone starts to sound the same.

An exceptional interview experience is more fun for the participants and sets you apart from everyone else, which is extremely valuable in today's job market. According to the American Bureau of Labor Statistics, between October 2024 and September 2025, the number of unemployed increased by 600,000. With many more eligible candidates entering the job market due to layoffs and economic factors, more people are applying to each role, and fewer interviews are leading to job offers.

So how do we make sure each interview is unique from the last and fosters a genuine connection? Sharing your challenges, mistakes, and failures makes interviews a lot more interesting for both parties. Who wants to hear about a project that went perfectly? Who would believe it went perfectly, or the only mistake made was so minor, it took you a day or less to solve? An interview is your opportunity to show what it's like to work with you, issues and all.

Being yourself helps earn trust. So be you. Trust yourself to show up authentically in an interview. It's the ultimate litmus test of whether the job is the right one for you.

The Enneagram & Job Interviews

During the pandemic I was building my company, Hire Possibilities, and I realized I loved the intersection of job interviews and the Enneagram: focusing on accepting yourself and highlighting strengths. I embarked on my own Enneagram journey (I'm a 6w5!) and devoured all the Enneagram books, workbooks, and podcasts I could find. I loved how the framework was validating, normalizing, and motivating to work with all at once.

One of my strengths is individualization, and one of the things I enjoy most is getting to know each of my clients as an individual so I can tailor my recommendations to their specific needs. After some time, I realized the Enneagram is a great way to customize this coaching at a larger scale, so clients don't necessarily need to work one on one with a coach.

To that end, this book blends interview coaching with the Enneagram to help job-seekers and hiring managers connect on a more human level. The Enneagram is a tool that helps you know yourself (and others) better. With roots in ancient spiritual traditions, the Enneagram was later integrated with modern psychology and evolved into a practical tool for understanding human motivation. While the Enneagram has recently gained popularity in Christian communities, my work featured in this book is completely secular and can be used by anyone, no matter their spiritual beliefs.

If you're an interviewee, the Enneagram can provide guardrails and reveal aspects of yourself you may not be aware of. It provides an outside perspective to understanding how you might be perceived in an interview. By showing up as fully you, including your flaws, you are more likely to make yourself memorable in an interview setting and end up in a role that feels like it was made for you.

If you're an interviewer, knowing your Enneagram type and how to apply it makes you more approachable. It isn't a hiring filter, but it will help you build awareness and empathy. Throughout this book, I'll point out ways to use it ethically in interviews.

When working with my clients, both job-seekers and hiring managers, I encourage them to reflect on and embrace their entire selves and career experiences. The focus is not on perfection, but on their flaws and the challenges they have overcome, to demonstrate their ability to earn trust with the customers and colleagues they'll be interacting with every day.

Sometimes candidates have a hard time showing vulnerability, either with me during the coaching process or during the interview itself. It may be difficult for them to see the unique "soft" strengths they bring to the role. They may consistently be called in to interview but never get the job. Often, they simply don't have the tools to identify their blind spots. Meanwhile, a hiring manager may struggle with leading an interview, selling the role, or gathering the information they need to assess a candidate.

This book isn't about how to be perfect; it's about rediscovering the value already buried in your unique experience. Imagine the Enneagram as an archaeological dig: Take the tools related to your type and gently chip away at your experience like an archaeologist unearthing a dirt-encrusted piece of pottery. As you remove the dirt, you may uncover parts of your experience you hadn't previously considered strengths, or you may become aware of blind spots that will help you get ahead of underlying assumptions. When you recognize that you're a work in progress and you are valuable, you can find success.

Knowing Your Enneagram Type

It's best to know your Enneagram type before we get started. While it's fun to take quizzes, these tests aren't always reliable. If you truly want to dive deep into the world of the Enneagram, you'll need to explore your internal motivations. If you're interested in using the Enneagram framework for personal growth beyond improving your interview skills, I recommend checking out the Rheti Assessment (www.enneagraminstitute.com).

To get the most out of this book, if you don't know your Enneagram type (or subtype), try this quick quiz.

Instructions: Read each question and circle the option (a–i) that feels most true for you, even if it isn't how you wish you were. When taking this quiz, some have asked if they should answer as their "real selves" or their "work selves" – go with your first instinct and what feels most true to your core beliefs. Responding as your work persona may cause you to veer in the direction of another type (especially 1, 2, 3 or 8), and that chapter may not be as useful to you when preparing for your next interview.

1. When you're under pressure, what feels most important to protect?
    a. Doing things the right way and maintaining integrity
    b. Being kind, helpful, and appreciated
    c. Being seen as capable, successful, or effective
    d. Staying true to your identity and feelings
    e. Preserving your energy, privacy, or independence
    f. Feeling prepared, secure, and supported
    g. Keeping options open and staying positive
    h. Maintaining control and not being vulnerable
    i. Keeping the peace and avoiding conflict

2. What tends to quietly drive many of your decisions?
    a. A sense of responsibility and improvement
    b. A desire to be needed or valued by others
    c. A focus on goals, results, or progress
    d. A longing for meaning and authenticity
    e. A need to understand before engaging
    f. A concern about what could go wrong
    g. A pull toward enjoyment, freedom, or possibility
    h. A drive to stay strong and self-reliant
    i. A wish for harmony and ease

3. When something goes wrong, what's your most natural inner reaction?
    a. It shouldn't be this way. How do I fix it?
    b. Did I let someone down?
    c. How do I recover or move forward quickly?
    d. Why does this always affect me so deeply?

e. I need more information before responding.
f. What risks did I miss?
g. There must be another, better option.
h. I'll handle this myself.
i. Let's not make this a bigger issue than it needs to be.

4. What feels most uncomfortable for you?
    a. Making a mistake or being morally wrong
    b. Feeling unappreciated or unwanted
    c. Being seen as unsuccessful or ineffective
    d. Feeling ordinary or misunderstood
    e. Feeling overwhelmed or overstimulated
    f. Feeling unprepared or unsafe
    g. Feeling trapped or limited
    h. Feeling controlled or powerless
    i. Feeling tension or disconnection

5. During a job interview, what are you most focused on?
    a. Giving accurate, flawless answers
    b. Being warm, likable, and supportive
    c. Presenting yourself as competent and impressive
    d. Being genuine and not misrepresenting yourself
    e. Not oversharing or being put on the spot
    f. Answering correctly and avoiding mistakes
    g. Keeping things engaging and upbeat
    h. Staying confident and not being intimidated
    i. Creating a comfortable, smooth interaction

Scoring: Count which letter you selected most often.

- Mostly a's → Enneagram Type 1– "The Reformer"

  Enneagram type 1s are disciplined, responsible and always want to do what's right. They believe processes can always be improved. 1s hold themselves and others to high standards of integrity and can be prone to black and white thinking.

  Watch out: If you answered this quiz thinking you need to "always give the perfect response" in a job interview, you could accidentally type yourself as a 1.

  The best way to know you're a 1: You have a relentless inner critic, and a strong sense of what you believe is right or wrong in every situation.

- Mostly b's → Enneagram Type 2 – "The Helper"

  Enneagram type 2s are considerate, focused on relationships and helping others. They identify the needs of their friends, family or team members, and do whatever they can to support them. Sometimes 2s feel resentment when they feel their loved ones aren't as considerate towards them, or don't appreciate their efforts.

  Watch out: Part of our culture's societal conditioning for women is to act more like a 2. If you find yourself trying to people-please in the workplace, you may accidentally type yourself as a 2.

  The best way to know if you're a 2: You have a gift of always knowing what others need, and consistently step in to help before anyone asks.

- Mostly c's → Enneagram Type 3 – "The Achiever"

  Enneagram type 3s are motivated by progress, accomplishments and recognition. These ambitious leaders typically exceed their goals and do very well in professional settings.

Watch out: If you're overly focused on packing your resume or interview with accomplishments during your job search, but you aren't an overachiever, you may accidentally type yourself as a 3.

The best way to know if you're a 3: You have an ever-growing list of awards, achievements and extracurricular activities you can't wait to tell everyone about.

- Mostly d's → Enneagram Type 4 – "The Individualist"

  Enneagram type 4s have a rich inner world and are motivated to understand themselves, apart from others. They are creative, unique, and emotionally attuned. They value originality and depth.

  Watch out: If you think that the best way to act in an interview is to stand out from other candidates, but the rest of type 4 descriptions don't resonate with you, you may have accidentally typed yourself as a 4.

  The best way to know if you're a 4: You've always felt a little bit different than everyone else, and authenticity is what you value most.

- Mostly e's → Enneagram Type 5 – "The Investigator"

  Enneagram type 5s are curious – they love learning, deep thinking and research. Very introverted and careful with how they spend their energy, they tend to be cautious rather than jump into action.

  Watch out: If you're an introvert who finds interviews exhausting (I feel you!), or you've been holding yourself back for any reason, you may accidentally type yourself as a 5.

  The best way to know if you're a 5: When you're out of energy for the day, you hit the wall and immediately require alone time or rest.

- Mostly f's → Enneagram Type 6 – "The Loyalist"

  Enneagram type 6s tend to think the world is a scary place and prepare for worst case scenarios. They seek security and take on a great deal of responsibility. Valuable members of their community, they prepare for issues that may arise and are loyal and committed to their teams and friends. Counterphobic (or One-to-one subtype, below) 6s reject their anxiety and face their fears, which may make it more challenging to identify their Enneagram type. It is believed that Enneagram 6 is the most popular personality type.

  Watch Out: If you have anxiety, you may accidentally type yourself as a 6.

  The best way to know if you're a 6: You always know where the emergency exit is, or have a plan for when the worst happens.

- Mostly g's → Enneagram Type 7 – "The Enthusiast"

  Enneagram type 7s are the life of the party – motivated by a desire for positive experiences, variety and adventures. They are the best person to have in a brainstorm with their quick thinking, optimism and ability to find the silver lining in any situation.

  Watch Out: If you feel like you need to come across as cool and flexible during an interview, or if you've had a hard time finding the right position and have bounced around from job to job, you might accidentally type yourself as a 7.

  The best way to know if you're a 7: You're constantly thinking about new ideas, possibilities and the exciting things that could come next.

- Mostly h's → Enneagram Type 8 – "The Challenger"

  Enneagram type 8s are driven by justice, upholding what they believe is right through strength and independence. They are comfortable being in charge and appreciate straightforward communication.

Watch out: If you believe showing up assertively in an interview is what matters most, you may accidentally type yourself as an 8.

The best way to know if you're an 8: You reject authority and believe you are at the helm in all situations.

- Mostly i's → Enneagram Type 9 – "The Peacemaker"

  Enneagram type 9s are harmony focused, and do not like tension. They foster a calm environment where others feel comfortable and included. Patient and kind, sometimes 9s can come off as too laid back or as procrastinators.

  Watch out: If you think you should do everything not to rock the boat during an interview, you may accidentally type yourself as a 9.

  The best way to know if you're a 9: You're conflict avoidant and often find yourself in a mediator role with friends and family.

If you're torn between two or three types, that's common. Your motivations can shift by context.

Enneagram Sub Type Quiz

1. When you walk into a job interview, what feels most important to get right?
   a. Making sure I'm fully prepared, composed, and unlikely to make mistakes. I want to feel steady and competent.
   b. Reading the room and understanding how I fit into the team or organization. I want to make sure I align.

c. Creating a strong impression and building a meaningful dynamic with the interviewer. I want there to be real chemistry.

2. In a job interview, I feel most unsettled when...
   a. I don't feel fully prepared or something catches me off guard.
   b. I can't quite read how I'm being perceived within the broader team context.
   c. The conversation feels flat or there's no real energy between us.

Scoring: Count which letter you selected most often.

- Mostly a's → Enneagram Self-Preservation Subtype
  The self-preservation subtype is most concerned with safety and maintaining stability. They can be quite practical and focused on themselves, compared to other subtypes.
- Mostly b's → Enneagram Social Subtype
  The social subtype is more focused on their social standing, observing and taking note of the group dynamics and shared values in all situations.
- Mostly c's → Enneagram One-to-One Subtype (sometimes referred to as Sexual subtype)
  The one-to-one subtype is focused on meaningful connection with other people or experiences. They are drawn to what feels engaging or transformative.

If you're finding this quiz tricky, or not quite resonating, you might also ask yourself, "which of these could I not live without?" - alone time (Self-Preservation), time with groups of people/community (Social) or one-on-one interactions (One-to-one)?

How to Use This Book

While you may want to immediately dive into the Enneagram, Part 1 of this book is focused on interview essentials to set the foundation for the concepts I mention throughout the rest of the book, so I encourage you to read it first.

Then, skip ahead to the chapter for your Enneagram type. If you still aren't convinced you know your type, read each Enneagram chapter or consider reading the chapters in this book that align with your top three possible Enneagram numbers to see what resonates most with you. Let curiosity be your guide, but you know yourself better than any personality quiz will, so you can determine what guidance is most helpful for you.

You may find certain parts of the chapter related to your Enneagram type more triggering than resonant. This is normal. That feeling may be pointing to a current gap in your awareness. Let it sit with you and see if the information resonates more as time goes by. If it doesn't, let it go.

There may be value in reading the chapters related to your other numbers: the number you go to in stress (you may act more like this type when under duress), the number you go to in growth (you may act more like this type when actively working on your personal growth or feeling comfortable with yourself), and your two wing numbers (the numbers on either side of your type in the Enneagram framework, which you might also strongly relate to). If you aren't sure what these numbers are, check out the table below. As an interviewer, you may find it valuable to read the chapters about the Enneagram types you want to hire for your organization, so you know what to look for or how to make those candidates feel more comfortable.

Enneagram Reference Chart (Core Dynamics per Type)

Type	Stress Arrow	Growth Arrow	Orientation to Time	Wing Options
1 – Reformer	4	7	Past (what should have been done better)	9 or 2
2 – Helper	8	4	Present (others' current needs)	1 or 3
3 – Achiever	9	6	Future (what's next / winning)	2 or 4
4 – Individualist	2	1	Past (longing/identity memory)	3 or 5
5 – Investigator	7	8	Future (preparing to handle what's coming)	4 or 6
6 – Loyalist	3	9	Future (anticipating risk)	5 or 7
7 – Enthusiast	1	5	Future (possibility + escape from present discomfort)	6 or 8
8 – Challenger	5	2	Present (what's happening right now/control)	7 or 9
9 – Peacemaker	6	3	Past (comfort/familiarity)	8 or 1

This book is not meant to be a replacement for deep personal Enneagram work or a "quick fix" for job interview skills. It's a lens through which to gain perspective. There are many books out there that provide a full synopsis of each personality type – this book is specifically tailored to job interviews, and assumes you know a little about your type already. If this is new to you and this book has piqued your interest in the Enneagram, I recommend reading any of the resources I've included in the last chapter of this book, as well as working with a therapist or a spiritual advisor. Working within your type is not a linear journey, so try to enjoy the process.

What to Expect from This Book

After reading this book, you'll feel more confident about showing up as a more authentic version of yourself. Here's an overview of what we will cover:

- The STAR Method and how to use and respond to behavioral interview questions for effective interviews
- The strengths you are bringing to your future team, so you can shine in hiring conversations
- Your interview "weaknesses" and how to embrace them and use them to your advantage
- Recognition of the value of working with team members of different Enneagram types
- Unconscious biases
- How to use information about your type to keep yourself going when the hiring journey gets tough
- Actionable takeaways you can use immediately to improve your interviewing skills

While I do want to make preparing for interviews more fun, I don't want to make light of the current job market. It's not just your perception; as of this writing, it is tough for both job-seekers and hiring managers. Beyond the obvious fact that most of us need a steady income to keep our rent or mortgages paid and food on the table, it is incredibly difficult to apply to hundreds of jobs without hearing back, to jump on dozens of phone calls or Zoom interviews without knowing why you aren't getting to the next step.

I have seen many clients waste hours of their precious time using AI for mock interviews (spoiler alert: it is not the same as working with a human), prepping scripted answers for the "most common" interview questions, and waiting by the phone for recruiters to call them back.

Many hiring managers choose the first candidate to enter the room out of desperation (I'm also guilty of this!), costing them money, time, and mental health before they finally go back to the drawing board to start the hiring process all over again.

My goal with this book and with using the Enneagram to scale job interview coaching is to save you a lot of time and money in the long run. As a hiring coach, I always want to be as efficient as possible when supporting my clients. This is meant to be a quick read, providing you with actionable tools you can begin to use immediately.

Before we talk about the differences between the Enneagram types, let's start by making sure we are working from the same foundation of job interview best practices. Please do not skip these important chapters, as the Enneagram-specific information builds upon it. After that, you might want to jump directly to your Enneagram number, to either the job-seeker or hiring manager section (or both!), and then circle back to the other types later.

How do you want to show up in your next interview? What would it look like if you could walk into an interview feeling calm, prepared, and entirely yourself? Let's explore how to bridge the gap between this future state and your current reality.

PART 1

Best Practices

CHAPTER 1

Behavioral Interview Questions & The STAR Method

AT 23, I walked into our company's large conference room with confidence, a long list of interview questions, and a big smile I hoped would camouflage the overwhelm I was feeling. Across from me was a hopeful young candidate who had applied to our open producer position.

I had recently asked my supervisors and clients to open an associate producer role for a key account I was leading at our digital agency. Working 90-hour weeks had turned out to be unmanageable, no matter how much yerba mate I drank or sleep I gave up. This became clear one afternoon when I opened the Notes app on my phone and found an incredibly helpful and detailed to-do list I had no memory of creating at 2:31 a.m. It was time for some support.

My managers approved my request, on the condition that I would lead the interview process with limited guidance. I was thrilled; how hard could it be to find the perfect person to delegate these day-to-day tasks to? (Spoiler alert: It turns out this is a very difficult task for someone with little career experience and no formal interview training.)

At the time, I thought the best way to prove how great I was at interviewing was to come in prepared with a lengthy list of questions. I interrogated the candidate to try to figure out how they would handle working with demanding clients in a high-pressure environment. I asked a lot of "What would you do?" hypotheticals, thinking they might slip up. Prior to the interview, I had briefly considered conducting an intense "test" that involved throwing sticky notes across the room in an angry client role-playing exercise (thankfully, I reconsidered this, as it didn't seem very kind).

I secretly hoped the more senior members of my team would make up for my lack of knowledge in this area, but they also had very little training and trusted my judgment. I had a track record of being a good judge of character, so I leaned heavily on my gut instinct and vibes with the candidate in the room without considering I was so desperate for relief, I'd hire anyone with a brain. Additionally, I had a strong, unrealized familiarity bias for candidates in the same demographics as me.

I hired the first person I interviewed. Our interview had remained extremely high-level: While I asked plenty of the basic interview questions (like "What are your strengths and weaknesses?" or "Do you know how to use Microsoft Project?"), the responses centered around basic functional skills that could be found in the job description or in a quick internet search for "how to answer common interview questions." I did not gather the amount of detail necessary to know if this candidate would truly be a good fit for the role. One of the main issues was my style of questioning in no way determined whether the candidate was being authentic or feeding me memorized, generic, people-pleasing responses. They seemed to have the skills necessary for the role, and their happy-go-lucky personality felt like a good "culture fit."

It seemed to be a great match at first, but after a few weeks of onboarding resulting in extra hours worked and emotional pain on both sides, I realized I had made the wrong decision. I still carry guilt that my lack of interviewing skills cost me, our company, and, perhaps most importantly, our new hire, precious time, money, and sanity.

A year or so later, when I started my next program manager (PM) role at a much larger tech company, we were required to take interview training before we could be a part of the interview process. There I learned about behavioral interview questions, and everything clicked. I fully understood why my previous methods hadn't worked. Once I learned how to effectively use this type of questioning, I never wanted to go back.

Behavioral Interview Questions

Credit for inventing behavioral interview questions goes to industrial and organizational psychologists from the 1970s who were looking for better evidence-based assessments. Behavioral interview questions ask job candidates to share examples of specific situations they've been in. An example would be "Tell me about your greatest professional achievement." The interviewer doesn't stop there, though; after the initial response from the candidate, they ask follow-up questions to gather more information so they can understand the full context of the situation.

An experienced interviewer knows which follow-up questions to ask (such as "It sounds like you were working closely with your team. Can you describe your specific contributions?" or "How did you and your company define success for that project and why?" or "What would you do differently if you could go back in time and work on this project again?") and how to create an environment where the candidate feels comfortable enough to honestly share all the relevant details of their experience. This is easier said than done, which is why many job-seekers feel nervous and unprepared for these types of questions.

Why do organizations use behavioral interview questions? Here are a few reasons:

1. They want to know how a candidate performed or handled an actual situation. Any candidate can describe what they would ideally do in a hypothetical state. In reality, it's unlikely everything could be handled perfectly.
2. Candidates often memorize scripts to prepare their responses to hypothetical questions. Asking behavioral questions will help prevent hiring someone based on a prepared speech that doesn't represent their performance.
3. These types of questions are best for measuring "soft skills" that are difficult to teach once someone is in the role. Companies want to know what to expect when a candidate will be the face of their project or account and work directly with clients.
4. Behavioral interview questions allow interviewers to dive deep into a particular area of focus and gather more information by asking follow-up questions.

To this day, behavioral interview questions are the foundation of my interview process. Over the past decade, I've watched them gain popularity in interviews across industries and roles. I always work with my clients (both job-seekers and hiring managers) on mastering behavioral interview questions. If you can learn to answer a behavioral interview question well, you'll gain the confidence to answer any type of interview query.

Behavioral interview questions are usually asked in the final rounds of an interview, once a candidate's primary functional skills have been assessed and they've been deemed capable of performing the day-to-day tasks of the role. These questions can still evaluate functional skills, especially if the interviewer drills into tools or actions taken by the candidate.

All the examples I will provide of interview questions to prepare for (or to ask) in interviews will be behavioral. If you're an interviewer getting ready for or reviewing your notes after an interview using behavioral interview questions, consider the following:

1. What values are an integral part of this role and/or company, and which questions most closely reveal those values?
2. What situational examples will best demonstrate a candidate would be a good fit for this role/company?
3. What strengths are associated with success in this role?
4. What type of "cultural archetype" might be most successful as a part of this team? (e.g., Hero, Nurturer, or Rebel)
5. What gaps may need to be filled by the candidate or company to get us closer to a true fit?

There are examples of behavioral interview questions sprinkled throughout each Enneagram chapter, as well as ten more bonus questions in the resources section at the end of this book.

The STAR Method

The STAR method grew out of structured behavioral interviewing research in the 1970s and 1980s and was popularized through corporate leadership assessment firms such as Development

Dimensions International (DDI). The best way for a candidate to initially respond to a behavioral interview question is by using STAR:

1. Situation: Candidate sets the scene and provides necessary details for context.
2. Task: Candidate describes what their responsibility was.
3. Action: Candidate explains exactly what steps they took to address and resolve the situation.
    a. The candidate should use the word "I" more than "we," as they should be describing their individual contribution.
4. Result: Candidate shares what outcomes their actions achieved.
    a. Consider if the interviewer and the candidate use the same system of measurement to judge success, as these may differ depending on the role or company.

If you are a job-seeker, I encourage you to spend some time thinking about examples you want to use in your interviews using this structure.

After the candidate provides their STAR response, the interviewer should continue to ask follow-up questions to gain clarity and understand how their answer may relate to the role being offered. This is why you should not simply memorize a scripted response in the STAR structure. As a job-seeker, you will be diving even deeper into the topic, so you need to be able to answer additional questions you couldn't have known in advance.

To further illustrate how this looks in an interview, here's my own example from my time as a senior PM at a large tech company:

Situation

I was the lead Product Imaging PM for a program called Human Context. The goal was to roll out over 200k images with dimensions against a human silhouette so customers wouldn't accidentally buy products that were the wrong size, like five-pound Hershey Bars (yes, these exist and trust me, they are difficult to eat!).

We received an escalation "question-mark email" from our CEO, as third-party sellers in the consumables category had been requesting customer service remove our images because they didn't like the way they looked, and we kept reuploading the images, unaware of the issue.

We had to educate third-party sellers about why and how we created the images to provide an accurate representation of the products for customers, as well as prevent this issue from happening in the future.

Task

As the lead for the program, I partnered with the consumables and customer service teams, who had differing points of view, to come up with a new process for addressing these requests.

We had to give customer service the ability to educate third-party sellers, letting them know the images and dimensions were accurate and we wouldn't be removing them.

We needed to send a response to our senior vice president as soon as possible.

Action

I led meetings between our groups and created flow charts and documentation for customer service.

I walked through our process with the customer service reps to make sure they understood it and they could work with third-party sellers to follow it.

I monitored weekly volume data even more carefully at the product level to ensure this wasn't still an issue.

I created a policy that detailed how retail and their support teams must communicate up front with customer service in the future to prevent issues like this from happening.

I wrote up the Product Imaging portion of the "question-mark email" follow up document, outlining the steps we were taking to resolve the issue.

Result

We were able to exceed our goal with over 242K images launched.

Customer service used our new process and documentation without issue.

We didn't receive any further questions from our CEO or our senior leadership after we sent the document. We quelled their concerns.

Entry Level Roles

Don't stress if the examples you're bringing to your next interview aren't as impactful or descriptive as these. I chose the previous model to illustrate the kind of detail I look for once a candidate has some experience under their belt. First time job-seekers might be intimidated by STAR. Here's an example of how to use this structure at a smaller scale:

Situation: We had a group capstone senior project at my university. With one week left in the semester, I realized my group members hadn't even started their portion. If we didn't submit our project on time, it could prevent me from graduating.

Task: I had to work with my classmates to ensure their portions of the project would be completed on time, without neglecting my other responsibilities.

Action: I scheduled an emergency meeting for the group. I uncovered the barriers preventing them from doing their work and created a plan to complete the project. I took on some extra work, but not all of it, to ensure we were successful.

Result: We submitted our project on time, and received a B+, which was a win given the condensed timeline. In the future, I would make my participation expectations clear at the beginning of the project and check in with my classmates throughout to streamline the process.

This structure may seem rigid at first, but after you get used to either answering questions using the STAR method or listening for each part of it in a candidate's response, it will come naturally.

These are foundational guidelines for interviewing, but this is an art, not a science. A candidate could provide the "perfect" responses to every question and still not be the right fit for the role. At the end of the day, whether you are an interviewer or a candidate, you want to share as much information as possible.

Throughout this book, you will hear me mention "yellow flags" and "red flags." A red flag from a candidate gives the interviewer immediate pause: It could be a legal concern (e.g., an inappropriate reference to race, gender, etc.) or an issue related to a soft skill that is extremely hard to teach, like earning others' trust and building relationships.

Yellow flags are responses from the candidate that seem like they could lead to a red flag and accordingly require follow-up from the interviewer. Examples of this could be referring to another team member as being hard to work with, leaving out critical details, or deflecting one of your follow-up questions.

Some interviewers stop their line of questioning when a yellow or red flag comes up, but I always recommend following the thread in a friendly and open way, so you can determine if it's truly a roadblock or simply a misunderstanding. The only time I recommend moving on or stopping the conversation is if the candidate says something blatantly illegal or inappropriate. Otherwise, it is not helpful to either the interviewer or the job-seeker to point out "wrong" or disagreeable answers.

As an interviewee, the best way to know you may have crossed the line into a yellow or red flag is by observing the interviewer's behavior: if their eyes widen, if they pause, if they stop you while you're talking, or if they quickly move on to another question. It is sometimes worthwhile to say, "I want to make sure I answered the last question adequately. Did anything I said not align with what you're looking for?" There is risk in being direct, but the risk of a wrong assumption may be higher. They may have glanced at the clock and realized they needed to move the interview forward, and you'll feel better looking back on the interview knowing you checked in.

In the following chapters, we will apply an Enneagram lens to this interview framework. The Enneagram shows us we're all valuable, imperfect, and uniquely motivated, and we'll show up to an interview in distinct ways. You will likely not be able to identify the type of person sitting across the table from you in a 45-minute interview, but by understanding how these types show up to an interview, you can increase your confidence and efficacy.

Reflection Questions

Before we dive in, I recommend taking some time to reflect on the following points to ensure you have a solid understanding of both behavioral interview questions and the STAR method. I find once my clients master the basics of these frameworks, they're confident they can walk into any interview and accomplish their goals.

Job-Seekers:

1. What are your favorite types of behavioral interview questions? Why?
2. What are your least favorite types of behavioral interview questions? Why?
3. Do you feel confident answering behavioral interview questions using the STAR method? Consider three example situations you could bring up during an interview, then practice talking about them in detail.

Hiring Managers:

1. What are your favorite types of behavioral interview questions to ask? Why?
2. What are your least favorite types of behavioral interview questions to ask? Why? Are your least favorite types still worth asking?
3. When you're interviewing a candidate, do you feel confident you can keep them on track using the STAR method to get the information you need?

CHAPTER 2

Unconscious Bias

AT THE END of the day, I was getting ready to interview a candidate for a PM position. Looking over a crisp, tailored resume, I suddenly noticed it, listed under "Certifications": "PMP – Project Management Professional." I audibly groaned. Most PMs I knew who were great at their job had natural executive function skills they brought into the role. They didn't need to work at being a PM; it was already who they were. Every PM I'd had a hard time working with had one thing in common: a PMP certification. Unsurprisingly, I was not inclined to hire the candidate.

I was surprised by the debrief with my colleagues after the interview. I was usually on the majority side of a decision after an interview, so I was shocked to find everyone but me was inclined to hire this candidate. My ego inflated by all the great interview feedback I had received recently, I figured the rest of the loop didn't do as thorough a job interviewing as I had. I shrugged and started reviewing the feedback.

No red or even yellow flags were found in anyone else's notes. I read and reread their written feedback, looking for any flaws to help me craft my argument, but I found none. This forced me to reconsider the interview and where I stood. Then it hit me: Of the last ten PM interviews I'd conducted, I had not been inclined to hire anyone. There were other issues with the candidates, sure, but at least half of my colleagues had been open to hiring them. What did they have in common? PMPs.

In a twist of fate, that same week, I had learned about unconscious bias: social stereotypes about certain groups of people that individuals form without realizing. Everyone holds unconscious beliefs about various identities, and these biases stem from one's tendency to organize social worlds by categorizing. (If you are interested in learning more about your own unconscious biases, check out Harvard's Implicit Associations Test: https://implicit.harvard.edu/implicit/takeatest.html)

If you're an interviewer, I invite you to take a closer look at the last group of candidates you passed on hiring. Did they have anything in common outside of concerns you may have had about their functional skills? Were there any commonalities among specific Enneagram types? Did they remind you of people with whom you tend to disagree or clash?

Learning about unconscious bias made me realize I had a bias against people with PMPs, and it was holding me back as an interviewer. As someone in a powerful position in the interview loop, I was keeping potentially great candidates from securing these roles. Yikes!

My bias stemmed from working with folks who had either been told they had to get a PMP to become a better PM, switched from another role to a PM, or decided to get a PMP certification because they weren't sure what else to do. I had always tried to stay on top of any biases related to demographics like gender, race, and religion—as much for legal purposes as for fostering diversity, equity, and inclusion (DEI)—but I had never considered I might be biased against something as innocuous as a PMP.

As you prepare to meet with a candidate, one of the most critical steps you can take as an interviewer is to check your conscious or unconscious biases, and that begins with awareness. To further address your biases, you can undergo Inclusive Leadership training or work with a mentor or coach on your specific goals. If you don't believe you can get past your bias in time to interview a candidate, you may be able to recuse yourself from the interview and ask an unbiased person you trust to replace you. If you are part of a small business, you may not have the option to ask someone to cover for your interview. Take the time to evaluate yourself and ensure you can objectively identify if a bias is blocking your ability to fairly interview a candidate. If you aren't confident in this, work closely with someone who can provide an objective viewpoint before moving forward with the frameworks within this book.

To address my own PMP bias, I made a point of reminding myself to be fair whenever I looked at a PM candidate's resume or sometimes even avoiding looking at the certifications list altogether. I didn't allow myself to make any judgments in that area; the recruiter and hiring manager had already considered certifications during their functional skills assessment, and I trusted their judgment.

Unconscious biases can affect job-seekers. Did you leave an interview feeling unsure if the job was a right fit because the person interviewing you didn't meet your expectations? Does seeing "DEI" in a job description (or not) make you feel a certain way about the company before you learn their official stance and policies? Did you not get an offer when you assumed the interviewer shared your values, resulting in an awkward faux pas?

Try to enter each interview with an open mind. Keep your responses as neutral as possible while staying true to your own experiences, and ask the dealbreaker questions that are vital to make the right decision for your career. Make it your goal to connect with whomever you're meeting with, even if you don't seem to have anything in common with them at first. This will increase your chances of success, as well as create a much more enjoyable experience for both of you.

Enneagram Biases

When working with a typing methodology like the Enneagram, be aware of any bias around "types" of people. You may be seeking an ideal personality or culture fit as you interview candidates, but you want to remain open to everyone you talk to, even if they don't seem to match the archetype you had in mind.

You might be interested in using the Enneagram to reduce your bias against a certain type of person, or maybe you've noticed your team lacks diversity in skills and personality traits. The point of using the Enneagram is to better understand and embrace all types and create more balance in your team, not to favor one or two types over all the others.

Keep in mind that it's not appropriate (or even possible) to "type" people you have a deep relationship with, much less someone you've known for all of 45 minutes. Always let the candidate tell you about themselves and check your assumptions at the door.

Even when using the Enneagram as a guide, don't expect to be able to perfectly predict how a candidate will fit within your current team's dynamics. Refer to Bruce Tuckman's Stages of Group Development (forming, norming, storming, performing) model when assembling or adding to a team. No matter what personality types are involved, conflict is normal and even essential to forming a successful and truly collaborative team. Knowing your team members' types, however, can allow you to anticipate some of the more common benefits and challenges you'll see as your organization grows.

Reflection Questions

Before moving forward, take a moment to write a journal entry or reflect on these questions related to unconscious biases:

Job-Seekers:

1. Are you aware of your conscious and unconscious biases and how they relate to your employment journey? How can you ensure they don't keep you from being offered the role you want?
2. Do you think unconscious bias may have affected your performance in previous interviews? What can you do to "play against type" or get ahead of any concerns interviewers may have in the future?

   [Note: It is the interviewer's responsibility to be aware of their biases, but it may be helpful to consider this when tailoring how you present yourself to recruiters and hiring managers.]

Hiring Managers:

1. Are you aware of your conscious and unconscious biases? Take the Harvard Implicit Associations Test, or evaluate your recent no-hire candidates for commonalities.
2. Before your next interview, cover up the name of the candidate. Do an initial review of their resume, cover letter, and portfolio. Ask yourself what gives you concern or pause. Is it related to a potential bias? If so, can you put that aside and give the candidate the benefit of the doubt during the interview? If not, is there someone who can take your place on the interview loop? What else can you do to counteract this bias moving forward?

CHAPTER 3

Job-Seeker Mindset & Preparation

Disclaimer: There may be times in your life when you need to get a job today to have a roof over your head and food on your plate tomorrow. If that is your current situation, you have nothing to be ashamed of, and I sincerely hope you find work soon. The following guidance is primarily meant for job-seekers who have the privilege of taking the time and space to reframe their mindset, who can be choosier or more intentional about the role that is the best fit for them. If possible, I always recommend searching for your next job while you still have your current one, but I realize that may not be the case in a job market littered with layoffs.

MY HIRE POSSIBILITIES client was frustrated. It had been months since he was laid off. He had applied for hundreds of positions he felt he was the perfect fit for, received callbacks for about ten, and was invited to a handful of in-person interviews. When you feel you're spending most of your time seeking out jobs and repeatedly throwing your resume and cover letters into the algorithmic void, it's only natural to feel frustration.

I explained to my client that the real problem is when these feelings infiltrate your mindset and create too much urgency or desperation. Signs of this are overpreparation, memorization, freezing in the moment, or putting too much pressure on yourself. This results in not being your authentic self during an interview, and by extension, not appealing to your interviewer. Or worse, you may try to be too vulnerable and share too much during an interview, which can be a real turnoff for the interviewer and end up costing you the role.

I challenged my client to think about how an interviewer could convince him the job was right for him, rather than the other way around. I encouraged him to come up with questions to ask and think about what answers would suffice. Simply looking at the interview process through this lens boosted his confidence and helped him bring a different version of himself to the next interview.

Think about a time when someone had a crush on you and you liked them back. Did they obsess over you, act overeager, or pressure you? Or did they get to know you in a relaxed way, without making you feel like everything hinged on you liking them back? My guess is your experience was closer to the latter; it's much more appealing to interact with someone who's self-assured than with someone who's clearly desperate for your approval.

Of course, this is not easy to do; I say this as someone who has absolutely been obsessed and awkward, both with crushes and jobs I really wanted. To say several things I've done in the past were cringeworthy is a gross understatement.

I remember being jealous of my friends who were so good at "playing cool" they always had their pick of dates or job opportunities. I couldn't figure out how to get there. If you want someone (or something, like a job) badly enough, it can be hard to stop ruminating about it. It was only when I realized I would be a great asset to any company and it was truly up to me to decide if I wanted a job or not that everything clicked into place.

In this chapter, we'll explore techniques you can use to remain appropriately excited but equally objective about prospective roles and interviews, which will help you attract the hiring managers and companies that are the best fit.

Overpreparation & Oversharing

As you work on your interview skills, keep in mind it is dangerously easy to overprepare. Do not memorize your responses to interview questions. Otherwise, the moment an unexpected follow-up question is asked, your confidence and your answers will weaken. I am always dismayed at "interview coaches" who teach their clients to memorize scripts or promise to reveal "what every interviewer wants to hear"; this is a false belief that leads to poor candidate experiences and feelings of inadequacy ("If this works for everyone else, why didn't it work for me?").

Here are three ways you can prepare for an interview:

1. While getting ready for your interview, consider a wide variety of behavioral interview questions and answers you can provide. Choose situations as recent and large in scope as possible, preferably ones you can talk about for 20 to 30 minutes each. If you have trouble remembering key details, use your prep time to take a closer look at notes, documents, or emails from that project. You can catch up with a colleague you used to work closely with or a friend you would vent to about the project. In the interview, don't be afraid to admit how your project went wrong or when you don't have an answer to something; paradoxically, this can create a more genuine connection with the interviewer.
2. If you're nervous about the one-on-one interview itself, consider practicing with a friend, family member, or interview coach. When working with people you have a personal

relationship with (or even ChatGPT), any feedback you receive may not be objective or helpful, so be sure to specifically ask for direct constructive criticism and let the other person know if there's a particular area you're focusing on.

3. Always have a goal for the interview within your control, so you don't lose hope over the course of what can be a months-long process. Your expectation of a successful interview should not be whether you get the job; it should be whether you and the interviewer were both able to determine if you were the right fit for the role. At the end of the interview, ask the dealbreaker questions that could prevent you from accepting the position. By avoiding a job that isn't the right fit for you, you are saving yourself and the company heartache and money. (In each chapter about Enneagram types, you will find suggestions of what questions you may want to ask an interviewer.)

However much or little you focus on your Enneagram type as part of your interview preparation, I want to be clear here: I do not recommend sharing this information with the interviewer unless you are specifically asked. If they ask you a question about self-improvement, learning, or growth, and this is an area you've spent a lot of time researching, then it may be appropriate to divulge this fact.

The reason I recommend not bringing up the Enneagram is your interviewer may not know what it is, and you may end up spending far too much of your interview time explaining it. Conversely, if they are aware of the Enneagram, this may trigger an unconscious bias they have about your "type." For example, they may assume you are not as flexible as they would like you to be in the role. The point of this framework is to discover new questions or aspects to focus on while preparing, not to put you in a specific box or overly narrow your focus.

While your type may typically be very strong in one area and weaker in another, every individual is unique; don't use this framework to create limitations. You are much more than your type, but using your type as a lens may allow you to see yourself differently— perhaps as someone meeting you for the first time might experience you. At the same time, don't overlook qualities you bring that may classically be strong in other types; for example, if you are a 2 but your sense of justice, especially related to those you care about, presents more like an 8, don't hold back! This is a strength that could make you a very valuable candidate in many fields, including, but not limited to, social work, education, and medicine.

When working through the gaps most common for your type, be sure not to overcompensate in other areas. In fact, I recommend you take ownership of the skills you're aware aren't your strongest. If you are asked a question that highlights an area of concern, call it out in your response: Talk about things you would do differently if you had a time machine and could go back to the situation you're discussing. Reference other situations, classes, certifications, or skills you've learned since to help bolster your shortcomings.

No one is perfect; everyone is a work in progress, including your interviewer. One interview for a particular job isn't going to make or break your career. If you continue to follow the path of lifelong learning, you will be in great shape.

Reflection Questions

Before moving forward, reflect on the following questions:

Job-Seekers:

1. Reflect on recent interviews. Have you felt more like a jilted lover than someone looking for your next job? Consider that you may need a mindset shift away from desperation to find the best-fitting role for you.
2. What is your goal for your next interview? Make sure it is within your control: meeting someone new, having a fun conversation, being authentic, asking a dealbreaker question about the role, etc.
3. What have you been doing so far to prepare for interviews? What has helped or hurt your performance? Create a preparation plan.
4. What is one action step you can take this week to improve your interview skills? Consider practicing with a friend or reflecting on a new behavioral interview question.

Read on to Part 2 for tips you can implement based on your type.

CHAPTER 4

Interviewer Mindset & Preparation

I ONCE OVERHEARD an acquaintance of mine who owns a small business bragging about how she would test job candidates. She talked about how she would act strangely to see if candidates would play along, show initiative, or avoid her entirely. In her mind, how they responded to trick questions or how well they were able to roll with the punches was the best indication of how successful they would be when partnering with her and her clients.

To her credit, it was a good test of how they'd feel about working with someone eccentric. But her philosophy fell more in line with "hire fast, fire faster." While she often found people she clicked with and who passed her tests, they didn't last in their jobs. Some of them were even so unsatisfied they were willing to take legal action against her. She was stumped; she thought she was doing everything right, as everyone seemed impressed with (or intimidated by) her process. Yet she didn't have the team to show for it.

Why Preparation Matters

There is a power dynamic in every interview that hiring managers should be aware of and use responsibly. Many professionals think they are bringing their best to the interview if they intimidate and test candidates, but this does not usually result in hiring the top candidates for the job. It is just as important, if not more so, for interviewers to consider their mindset and prepare thoroughly for each interview, just as interviewees do.

Consider that you are the candidate's first impression of your company. They will understandably be nervous, so to connect with them on a level that will reveal their true character, you first need to help them feel comfortable.

Show a candidate you genuinely care about them as a person first: Ask if they need a restroom break or a drink, or take a moment to ask about their day before beginning the interview. Make sure they know it is their job to evaluate you and ask you questions to know if they will be suited to the role. Think about your body language: Be open and friendly, lean forward, and show the candidate you are interested in what they have to say.

As an interviewer, you might be just as nervous, especially if you're not experienced yet, and that's perfectly okay! In fact, sharing your nerves with the candidate may help you develop a natural connection.

If used properly, behavioral interview questions can provide similar results to "testing," but with a much better candidate experience. While case studies, brainstorms, and coding tests, when proctored in a fair and kind manner, can be helpful for better understanding how a candidate thinks, intentionally putting a candidate in an impossible or high-pressure situation will only create an environment of distrust and unease.

Behavioral interview questions, on the other hand, can show you how a candidate handled a situation in the past, which is the best indicator for what they will do in the future. You should aim to ask only two or three behavioral interview questions in a 45- to 60-minute interview. This means you will need to ask the right follow-up questions to hear the full story and get the information you need.

Before each interview, use this process to ensure you're prepared:

1. Look at the candidate's resume, their LinkedIn™ profile, their writing sample, and any other information you may have.
2. Check yourself for biases. If you find any, consider them and ask yourself if you can still fairly conduct the interview. If you think you can, be aware of the bias while talking to the candidate and when writing up notes afterward. If not, find someone else to conduct the interview in your stead.
3. Reflect on the functional skills and values you want to prioritize to understand if the candidate is qualified. Ask three or four follow-up questions in this vein during the interview, and prepare an extra question or two in case you decide to shift mid-conversation.
4. Be aware of the power dynamic in the interview and plan to properly set the tone to ensure you can establish a connection.
5. Remind yourself that even if the candidate ends up not being hired, the interview is still a good use of time and will lead to the best outcome for both the candidate and the company.

After the interview, if you are feeling "on the fence," it's a no— and that's okay. Hiring the wrong person is painful, not only for the company in terms of cost and time, but also for the candidate. Run through your notes again and be sure that if it's a no, you have hard evidence to back up your decision based on the values and functional skills you are assessing.

If you find you often do not have all the information you need after an interview, remember the process takes time and practice. Don't be afraid to seek out support or coaching, as this is a skill that can come in handy in many aspects of your life!

Reflection Questions

Before moving on to the next chapter, take a moment to reflect on the following:

Hiring Managers:

1. Reflect on your recent interviews. Did your assessment match those of the other interviewers? Why or why not? Is there anything you want to do differently moving forward?
2. What behavioral interview questions can you ask to set yourself and the candidate up for maximal success in the interview? (If you need new question inspiration, read on!)
3. Are you in the middle of a particularly difficult hiring process? How could you improve the experience for the candidates and your interview loop?

Now that we've covered the basics, let's dive deeper into how to use the Enneagram to find your next great hire.

PART 2

Implementing the Enneagram

CHAPTER 5

Enneagram 1 – The Reformer

"Management is doing things right; leadership is doing the right things."

—Peter Drucker

IT WAS MY first phone screen after completing my interview training, and I was thrilled. We were so excited to speak to this candidate; she had great design skills and an interest in development. User Experience (UX) methodology was starting to catch on, and this candidate could be critical to our success in expanding our capabilities.

I was incredibly nervous and in my head. I was representing a huge tech company, and the fact that I had never successfully interviewed and hired anyone before gave me impostor syndrome.

As hard as I tried to pay close attention to the candidate's responses to my questions, my inner critic would not shut up.

"What did you just say? She can tell you're nervous."

I gritted my teeth and shoved the thought from my mind. I continued taking notes and trying to be present, listening to the candidate's calm and assured responses.

"She's not answering the way you thought she would. What are you going to ask next?"

I stumbled as I asked my follow-up questions and even "facepalmed" once (which I only did since the candidate couldn't see me over the phone).

"You're supposed to be a level higher than her. She's not going to respect you when you hire her. You're not getting the information you need."

Over the entire course of the 30-minute interview, the voice didn't stop. We did end up hiring the candidate, and she was everything we had hoped for, but my inner critic never left. For years afterward, every time I interacted with that employee, our interview would come back to haunt me. My social anxiety got the best of me; I wondered if I had made a bad first impression we couldn't recover from.

Most of those fears were only in my head, of course; I doubt she would even remember the small mistakes I'd made on that first phone call. But they did impact our interview and our connection. The inner critic—impostor syndrome's best friend—can be detrimental to the interview process if you let it.

While many Enneagram books start from type 9, I think it's appropriate to kick off this book with type 1: a type who can be prone to the inner critic or black-and-white thinking about an interview performance, which can make or break an interview. This type may find it takes more time to get comfortable with the process or to stop judging themselves along the way. It may be hard for them to come to terms with the fact that there isn't always a "right" or "wrong" answer to an interview question.

Whether 1s are asking or answering the questions, they should try to be more objective and limit their natural judgment. They should avoid overpreparation and find confidence within themselves to ask or answer interview questions, rather than memorizing a script that won't show their authentic self.

To help soothe a 1's nerves and improve their mindset, it may be helpful to consider these practices:

1. Actively seek "shades of gray." At the end of the day, 1s should pick one interaction they may be judging as good or bad. Try to find the "gray" in the situation. With practice, it will be easier to see through a "gray" lens when considering others' actions and their own.
2. Name the inner critic. If you're a 1, what does your inner critic sound like? Are they male or female? Old or young? Someone you know or someone you don't recognize? Separate this inner voice from yourself. That way, when you leave an interview and you hear, "*Wow, you really blew it,*" you can question the thought or dismiss it: "Oh, hi, Nelly. I did my best in that interview and achieved my goal of learning more about the company. Let's let them tell us if I'm a fit for the job." The more you do this outside of an interview, the easier it will be to convince your inner critic to step aside in the moment.

Job-Seekers: Responding to Interview Questions

Black-and-white or judgmental thinking can be detrimental during an interview. Once, I was part of an interview loop for a candidate who had a PhD. Meanwhile, my highest degree is a bachelor's from a state university, and most of my learning has been through actual business experience. I was the only person on the loop for this position who did not have an advanced degree, and my role was to evaluate how the candidate would work with stakeholders from other teams.

At the beginning of the interview, the candidate asked me directly why I was part of the loop. I explained I could help answer any questions they might have about the company at large. The candidate said they did not understand how someone without a PhD could evaluate them, and they refused to answer my questions. I gently reminded them my experience with them would impact the ultimate hiring decision, as they would be working with other stakeholders who did not have PhDs, and I asked that they engage in a conversation with me. Still, they refused. To ensure a good candidate experience, I spent the rest of the interview answering their questions about the organization.

Now, I certainly don't know this candidate's Enneagram type, and this is an extreme example, but they displayed very rigid thinking and, perhaps unsurprisingly, they were not offered the role. While I doubt you would be this rude in your own interview, be sure not to judge your own responses or those of the person you're talking to, or you may end up holding yourself back from connection and opportunity.

Question that may be easy to answer:

"Can you walk me through a process improvement you've implemented?"

If Enneagram 1s back up and examine an existing process, they are often the first person to find steps that do not add value. They do this naturally when trying to create sanity around their own processes or trying to figure out what is bothering them about the way a team member is tackling a task. Looking at a map of a process, 1s can flex their right-versus-wrong thinking to fix problems they identify. It may be easy for them to think of several examples where something was "wrong" and they were the only one who could see how to make it "right."

If you're a type 1, you will want to make sure you're discussing an example of large enough scope for the role or team you're interviewing for. If you find yourself thinking of another instance mid-stream in an interview, don't panic! You can save that example for another question later. It may not be a "perfect" response, but it will give the interviewer what they're looking for, and your next example will be even stronger.

Question that may be more difficult to answer:

"Can you tell me about a time your colleagues thought something was good enough, but you didn't agree?"

This question is likely to trigger frustrating memories of when a 1 may have felt like they were the only sane person in the group, like they could have stopped the train wreck, but the conductor didn't listen. Answering this question will require balance, as they want to demonstrate their commitment to quality standards, as well as their ability to compromise or work with a group with differing opinions.

The key is not letting any resentment or rigidity leak into their responses. If a 1 feels like this may be difficult, they should do some work on their own to process their feelings before the interview. They could do a hard workout while actively thinking about the project, journal for twenty minutes each day over the course of a week, or ask a therapist, coworker, or friend if they are available to listen and provide an outside perspective.

If you're a 1, don't be afraid to be vulnerable in your response to this question. Do you wish you had acted differently? Did you realize those team members cared about quality, just not to the same degree you did? Could you have communicated your recommendations more effectively? Share this information with your interviewer so they can better understand how you think about the situation now versus in the past.

Subtypes

Let's consider how subtypes can impact a 1's performance in an interview. If you're a 1 and don't know your subtype, consider which of these three options resonates most with your experiences.

Self-preservation 1s may be most worried about how the interview is going to go and are most likely to have perfectionist qualities. They may appear more rigid, trying to control the interview as much as they can. They may be especially hard on themselves when discussing a mistake they've made— if they feel open enough to talk about it at all. If this is you, try to avoid bringing up examples that stir up resentment toward past customers or team members or make you feel like you were carrying all the weight of the project yourself, unless these are the only examples of appropriate scope to share. If you feel yourself becoming irritable with the interviewer at any time, take a second to breathe before responding.

Social 1s may easily fall into a trap of presenting themselves as overconfident or superior to others. They may not have many examples to share of collaborating with a team or adapting flexibly to change or feedback. If you are a social 1, lean into your confidence during the interview, but pay attention to how it's landing with the interviewer. Know what your tolerance for collaboration is. A director of mine once reflected to me, "Some PMs are team-focused and want to collaborate with other PMs, and some are mercenaries who just try to get the job done at any cost. I think you're team focused." I had never really considered this, as it was always expected I would be collaborating with other team members to be successful; however, I'd often find my achievements separated me from other PMs. I realized I could flex in different settings, but I was happiest when I could work independently, and I used that as a guide when looking for future roles.

One-to-one Enneagram 1s probably have examples where they identified issues with their teams or processes and asserted themselves to fix them. They may believe they know what's best for their project, team, coworker, or customer, and they may present as closed off to differing feedback. They may be more likely to go for roles they are not 100 percent qualified for, which gives them an advantage over similar candidates who might hold themselves back from taking risks. If you are one-to-one, use your forceful energy to spotlight your greatest accomplishments. Try to show a willingness to learn and become more flexible. You may be especially adept at convincing the interviewer you're suited for the role.

For all subtypes, tap into your 9 wing by not rocking the boat during the interview. Pay close attention to your interviewer and note any friction that comes up. You can certainly disagree if warranted, but try not to become too self-righteous in the interview, and remain open to differing perspectives to keep the peace and connection strong.

Tap into your 2 wing by assessing what the interviewer is looking for and showing them how you're going to provide it when they hire you. Demonstrate you have the answers to their biggest problems, and they can't afford to not offer you the role.

When you're stressed and find yourself sliding into the Enneagram 4 space, turn any frustration or melancholy you may feel about a particular situation into a chance to demonstrate your passion behind the topic. Did your team members frustrate you when they didn't take customer concerns as seriously as you did? Show your interviewers you won't let such apathy slide when you're in the role.

If you're feeling confident and secure during the interview, you may find yourself acting more like a 7, easily keeping the conversation flowing. Just be sure not to lose any credibility by softening your approach too much; continue to answer the interviewer's questions with rigor.

As an Enneagram 1, your orientation to time is the present, which will allow you to remain focused on the task at hand during an interview. Verbal processing is a product of this, so it can be helpful to know what you're trying to accomplish with each of your STAR examples to keep your responses streamlined. When you are in stress (in 4), you may find yourself thinking back to your past interviews, especially if you didn't feel like you performed well. Do your best to remain in the present while discussing the past work examples you're most proud of with your interviewer.

If you're feeling confident and growing into 7, you may find yourself speaking as if you have already been offered the role, putting yourself in imaginary future scenarios. Unless they've specifically asked you to do this, try not to assume this will be the outcome, no matter how well the conversation is going.

When connecting with an interviewer, loosen up your body posture to show you are open. Look as relaxed as you can; too much rigidity in your body language can make an interviewer wonder if you are that stiff all the time. Before the interview, squeeze in a tough workout or have an impromptu dance party at home or in your car. Your body will naturally relax a bit after moving some nervous energy out of the way.

Questions to Ask the Interviewer

As you wrap up the interview, consider asking these questions:

"How much of the process is already defined, and how much needs to be created?"

Enneagram 1s may be looking for opportunities to carve out and define new processes, rather than simply following what currently exists. If a 1 is expected to unquestioningly follow an existing process, they will not feel as valued as they would if their manager regularly asked for their feedback or assigned them to take the lead creating a new process. If the team is new or looking for a fresh perspective, there will be plenty of opportunities for a 1 to influence their day-to-day experience.

"What level of influence would this role have in cross-departmental decisions, especially regarding standards of quality and customer experience?"

A 1 can be empowered if their hiring manager expects them to represent the team and weigh in on improvements that would result in better customer experience or a higher quality of work. While these decisions are largely subjective, they can feel black-and-white to a 1, who needs to feel like they have a voice. If a 1 feels let down by the response to this question or determines they would be more of a follower than a peer or a leader, the role may not be right for them.

"What kind of support does the company provide for employees to make independent decisions that benefit both customers and team members?"

Enneagram 1s need to feel like they can keep moving forward without checking in with their manager or the team about every decision. It is paramount that their managers trust in their decision-making skills and give them room to make independent decisions. If every small decision needs to go through a check point, such as a manager, a skip-level manager, or a senior leader, this could make a 1 feel undervalued, like anyone could do their job.

If you are a 1 and the interviewer can provide examples that demonstrate they will fully trust you, that's a good sign you will be seen as helpful in this role and supported when issues arise. If the examples are weak and related to maintaining the status quo, you may want to reconsider and seek out another position or company that will better allow you to take charge and demonstrate your skills.

Given a 1's high quality standards and attention to detail, industries and roles for Enneagram 1s to consider include Compliance, Quality Assurance, Process Improvement, Accountant, Military or Law Enforcement, Building Inspection, and Technical Writing.

Reflection Questions

As you prepare for upcoming interviews, take a moment to reflect on these questions and next steps:

1. Has your inner critic negatively impacted your interviews? Can you name it and ask it to step aside for your next interview? The interviewer is not looking for perfection.
2. Do you have any good examples of past performance that demonstrate your flexibility and collaboration skills? Make a note of them for your next interview.
3. What are some dealbreakers for your next job? Look for autonomy and opportunities to uphold high quality standards and improve processes in your next role.
4. How much time have you spent preparing for interviews in the past? Limit the amount of time you spend so you don't overprepare and avoid memorization.

Hiring Managers: Asking the Interview Questions

I was part of an interview loop where a creative director was convinced the designer we were interviewing was the right fit based on his portfolio, a single quick phone screen, and the recommendation of a colleague she trusted. However, during the debrief session, we could see from the candidate's past interviews that there were some red flags that needed to be discussed before making a hiring decision. When anyone voiced concern, the creative director's body tensed and her eyes narrowed; she didn't even want to consider any red flags. She had been trying to fill the role for three months, and at this point, she was desperate to delegate work to an experienced employee so she could avoid burnout.

For the first 15 minutes of the debrief, the hiring manager wouldn't listen to team perspectives, insisting the candidate must have had "off" interviews with everyone else and the data the team had collected couldn't possibly be valid. As part of the required debrief process, she had to spend the next 15 minutes allowing other team members to share their perspectives, and even though it was frustrating for her, she came to understand the candidate probably wasn't the best hire for the team after all.

This is one of the dangers of being a type 1 interviewer: It's easy to shut out a candidate you don't think is good enough, and it's just as easy to fixate on a candidate you do.

Earlier in this book, I mentioned biases, both conscious and unconscious. As an Enneagram 1, you may be more susceptible to these biases and end up falling into the trap of deeming a candidate's responses "good" or "bad" too soon. Recognize that overcoming your biases is lifelong work and take the time to investigate the lenses you use to view the world.

Enneagram 1s may struggle more than others to get the amount of information necessary to determine if a candidate is appropriate for the team and role. If this is you, you may consider a candidate's unexpected answer a yellow or red flag that would prevent you from hiring them. You may be tempted to react mid-answer and give the candidate pause. This cuts off any chance you have of learning more about the candidate's thought process and whether or not your instincts about them are right.

Interviews should not feel like interrogations or judgment. Enneagram 1s may be more likely to rapidly ask candidates questions to show off their interview skills or test candidates by putting them in high-pressure situations. They often don't realize they're doing this; they're simply doing their best to find the right person for the job.

Think about how stressful it feels to be interviewed. The more you can train yourself to be open to all responses, the better the connection you will be able to make with the candidate, and the more information you will obtain with which to make your decision. Think about the candidates who may have been a great fit for your team but whom you passed up when you judged them too quickly. Think about all the time that judgment may have cost you in the long run.

When considering each candidate's responses to your questions, try not to think, "how would I have answered this?" That may lead you astray while you're trying to build a diverse team. Instead, ask yourself about any other details you would have liked to hear from the candidate. Did you miss out on asking for those details because you didn't think to ask? Did they avoid your question or go in an unexpected direction?

Notice when you feel like you're "clicking" with a candidate. Is it because you're truly connecting, or are they saying only what you want to hear? If it's the latter, they may be a "yes" person or a replica of yourself. Someone with a mindset like yours can make a great successor or assistant, but if you're building out a team, you'll likely want someone who can offer a different perspective.

If a candidate is otherwise a great fit but you wish they shared your skills for making quick decisions and following rules, consider writing up more documentation for them to review when they start or adding more training and mentorship opportunities to their onboarding plan.

Subtypes

Let's consider how subtypes can impact your performance as an interviewer. If you don't know your subtype, consider which of these three options resonates most with your experiences.

Self-preservation 1s may share the struggle I mentioned at the beginning of this chapter: silencing the inner critic during an interview. If you're a self-preservation 1, try your best not to worry about interviewing the candidate perfectly, as this will only get in the way. There isn't room at your interview table for a third person (even one who only takes up space in your head).

Social 1s may panic if a job-seeker takes their answer to a question in an unexpected direction. If you're a social 1, let the candidate finish their thought, then gently steer them back on track.

If they have a good first impression with a candidate, one-to-one Enneagram 1s may feel tempted to lead the candidate with their questions or hint as to what kind of response they're looking for. If you're a one-to-one Enneagram 1, avoid this instinct and allow the candidate to answer for themselves. Resist the urge to give the candidate feedback about how they can perform better in the next interview.

If you have a 9 wing, consider times when you have been able to be a little more easygoing or deliberately move more slowly. Make sure you aren't distracted by what happened right before the interview or what will happen after.

If you have a 2 wing and you're in a "loop interview" setting, ask the candidate if they need a break or something to drink. Tap into your caretaking tendencies. Showing you care about them as a human being will help foster connection and comfort that will make the conversation more fruitful.

Enneagram 1s move to 4 in stress. When you're hiring, this may come out if you feel the interview is tanking 20 minutes in and the next 40 minutes will be a waste of your time. If this happens, you may become moody or pull away from the conversation. Even if this candidate does not seem good for this role, they could still surprise you before the meeting is over, and at the very least, you're one step closer to hiring someone. If you still deem them unfit by the end of the interview, reflect without blaming yourself and overthinking about what you could do differently next time.

If you're a confident interviewer and you're enjoying talking to a candidate, you may find yourself shifting to 7. While this is great for connecting, make sure you ask the right questions and don't skip any necessary follow-ups during the interview, or else you may end up kicking yourself while reviewing your notes later when you find the candidate isn't measuring up on paper.

With your orientation to time in the present, you are good at being in the moment with a candidate. If you are feeling stressed during an interview, you may find yourself comparing the candidate to previous candidates; resist the urge to do this and anchor yourself in the moment by focusing on what this candidate is saying. I don't believe it's ever helpful to compare candidates to each other (it's fairer to compare them to the job description and expectations), but if you're going to do that, save it for when you're reviewing your notes. Each candidate deserves your full attention.

When talking to a candidate, try to make your body language as open and relaxed as possible. You might default to crossing your legs or arms or staring at the candidate throughout the interview. Keeping an open posture will have the reverse-engineering effect of making you feel more open to the candidate's responses.

Interviewing Other Types

If you are a 1 looking to diversify your team, you may want to consider looking for someone with a type 6 personality. These loyal and cautious team members can help balance conversations by playing devil's advocate. They weigh their decisions carefully, especially when it comes to relationships with others. This can be helpful for a 1, who may sometimes forge ahead in their decisions without fully considering how they'll affect everyone else.

You may want to consider a 7; they can help you question if your standards are too rigid, and they can increase morale when you don't have the energy for it. They can serve as the person on the team who schedules celebrations and provides the optimistic perspective in the board room.

Be on the lookout for any biases when you talk to candidates who fit the 8 or 5 personality types. You may consider an 8 abrasive or a threat at first, rather than an ally who will champion your team's efforts, even when you disagree. You may be frustrated with a 5's interest in gathering information before acting when you have already determined what the "right" decision is. Give them a little time and space to fill in any gaps you might not have seen yourself.

Reflection Questions

In your next interview, reflect on these tips to improve your performance:

1. When considering candidates to hire, what is your ratio of "inclined" to "not inclined"? If you are a no-hire vote more than 75 percent of the time, you may want to take a step back and ask if your standards are reasonable. It may be helpful to ask your mentor or trusted peers for feedback, especially if they have been in the same interview loops. You need to find a candidate who will be successful in a role, but you don't want to be overly picky.
2. Do you shut down a candidate if they answer your question differently than you expected? Keep the candidate talking by smiling and remaining open, even if it feels like they're digging their own grave. Think of yourself as a journalist who needs as many quotes as possible for a story.
3. Have you already decided you're hiring someone (or not) halfway through the interview? Don't judge yourself or the candidate before the interview is over. Let yourself be surprised by the outcome or where the conversation takes you.

CHAPTER 6

Enneagram 2 – The Helper

"No one has ever become poor by giving."

—Anne Frank

ONE OF THE things I loved about working for a big company was we had the opportunity to meet people from different teams and learn about various industries and roles. I found a position that I thought was a great fit for me, even though it was firmly in the retail space, as I had previously been working on internal teams supporting retail. To succeed in the role, I'd need to learn entirely new systems and tools and ramp up immediately. Unsurprisingly, the hiring manager was looking for a candidate with ten years of experience in the industry or more.

Eager to show I would fit in, I bent and contorted my examples in ways I thought would adequately answer the interviewer's questions. As the person in this role would be integrated with a large team, I gave examples where my team and I had all worked together to achieve a common goal. When I was pressed to talk about projects I'd led, I went for an angle of indispensability—without me, I said, the projects would have failed. I was worried any gap would be a red flag, so I tried to get ahead of their concerns by being a "yes person."

I was attuned to what the interviewer was looking for, and I thought I was using my emotional intelligence to mirror them, but it didn't work. Not only were my gaps still obvious, but my answers didn't highlight my real strengths or give a genuine picture of what it would be like to work with me. Had I admitted to my shortcomings and given examples demonstrating my success in my current industry without direct previous experience, I would have given the interviewer a more accurate representation of the value I could add to their organization.

As a 2, it can be easy to lose yourself in the process of supporting and focusing on others. This can be a good thing at work or in your community, but it can hold you back when you're trying to convey how you—an individual with your own skills and needs—would show up in a role.

Practice separating yourself from your former team members to specifically highlight what you've accomplished yourself but ensure you aren't coming across as single-threaded or suggesting your former company would have collapsed without you.

To help soothe your nerves and improve your mindset, it may be helpful to consider these exercises:

1. Spend time around someone who adores you and wants to take care of you. You're probably used to thinking about the ways you can best serve others in your life. Find a partner, friend, family member, or mentor who can help you on your hiring journey. It may be hard to accept this support, but they can make sure you aren't burning out from taking care of everyone else. For job-seekers, this will help with any rejection sensitivity that comes from not getting the roles you interview for. You'll always have someone to tell you how amazing you are!

2. Brainstorm circumstances where you advocated for yourself in the workplace. This will help you come up with STAR examples to share, and it can help protect you against falling into group think during an interview debrief. You're worth showing up for and you can support yourself in the workplace, even if your views differ from others'.

Job-Seekers: Responding to Interview Questions

She tapped her finger on her chin, deep in thought. I tried to keep her comfortable by averting my gaze to look down at my notes. I had just asked a candidate who was up for a leadership position about how she'd solved a problem, and she'd talked about how their team had tackled the issue. I'd then asked her to identify what she specifically had contributed to the solution, but she was drawing a blank.

"We had to put together a document."

I nodded. "Great! Can you talk about how you thought through the document? I'd love to hear more about the process."

"Yes! We thought that it needed to cover—"

"No, I'm asking what *you* did." I hated to interrupt her, but this was the tenth time she'd said "we," and our time was running out. "Can you try using 'I' statements? It sounds like you're very collaborative, which is great, but I'd like to know more about your specific contributions."

"I'll do my best," she assured me, sheepishly. "But we all worked very closely together, and I don't really like to brag."

Hard as she tried to fulfill my request, the rest of the interview was painful. Her team had been so cohesive she couldn't seem to remember what had been done by her versus by someone else. Once she got into a groove and relaxed into her "I" statements, the other problem became clear: She had been so integrated in her team she hadn't set her team members up for success; whenever she called out sick or otherwise wasn't available, the team suffered in her absence.

Enneagram 2s face a delicate balance between supporting other team members and codependency, which can make teasing out the details of a project more challenging for interviewers. Often, female 2s suffer societal conditioning to play the martyr or to take on more administrative or supporting roles, which can cause problems as well.

Question that may be easy to answer:

"Can you tell me about a time you helped a team member without being asked?"

This question about ownership highlights the most positive aspects of an Enneagram 2. They are the best equipped to identify if someone on their team is having a hard time or could use their support. If you are a 2, talk about a time when you jumped in to help get a project done before a deadline or noticed the team required a morale boost to stay motivated.

It needs to be clear to the interviewer whether the team member in question accepted your help or resisted it; you can use an example of the latter, but exercise caution, as it could show overstepping. What was the result of your help? How did you measure success? Would you do the same in a similar situation in the future, and why or why not? What did you learn from helping this team member?

Question that may be more difficult to answer:

"Can you tell me about a situation in a past role that made you angry?"

Prioritizing others' emotions and needs over your own is common if you're a 2, so you may feel uncomfortable talking to an interviewer about a difficult emotion such as anger. During the actual conflict that made you angry, you may have chosen to stuff your feelings inside rather than process them or use them to create a healthy boundary. If you are less self-aware, hidden resentment may come out while you are answering this question. You may have a hard time thinking of an appropriate example at all.

Give an example with a healthy and productive outcome for you, your customer, your manager, and your team. Instead of "seeing red for months after," think of a situation where you were mildly annoyed and had to steer your organization toward success. Try to choose an example that happened long enough ago that you don't need to verbally process it with your interviewer, since you've likely already vented to a trusted friend or therapist.

Subtypes

Let's consider how subtypes can impact your performance in an interview. If you don't know your subtype, consider which of these three options resonates most with your experiences.

Self-preservation 2s may need to check and see if they are presenting as mature or experienced enough for their role; they may be used to coming across as youthful, which can backfire in an interview setting, especially for mid-level or senior roles. They may be more sensitive to rejection. Shying away from the spotlight of an interview setting, they may fail to connect with the person evaluating them. Outside of the interview itself they should create scaffolding of support to encourage them in their preparation and provide constructive feedback if they need it. A friend or family member can remind them they are still valuable, even if they don't get the job.

An interview is a more comfortable place for a social 2, who is used to working to impress others. They may bring a strong network with them, which can be a great advantage for certain roles and industries. Their vulnerabilities can be used to their advantage in an interview by bringing a narrative that feels well crafted; however, they may need to work a little harder to make sure it feels authentic to the interviewer. They should test out their STAR examples on friends or family to verify they land as intended.

Unsurprisingly, one-to-one Enneagram 2s do best in one-on-one interview settings, where they can use their natural charm to connect with the interviewer. Their resume may hint at bouncing from job to job—perhaps they fell in love with the idea of another job, industry, customer, or colleague. They may sometimes be presented with a job offer after an interview, only to realize they never actually wanted the job, just the validation of the offer. They should be objective and realistic about their needs and what they are looking for in their next role. Sometimes there are valid reasons to pursue more roles and interviews, especially if it means building a network, finding a mentor, or learning about a new space. If this applies to you, make this clear to the interviewer up front (or in your cover letter) to avoid an incorrect perception of flightiness based on a busy-looking resume.

If you're a 2, tap into your 1 wing by seeking out or highlighting opportunities for process improvements that would benefit the entire team or company. Use the discernment of your 1 wing to influence where you take the conversation while upholding high standards for yourself.

Tap into your 3 wing by identifying your accomplishments before the interview and reveling in your strengths. Proudly assert yourself and talk yourself up in the interview.

When you find yourself going to 8 in stress, be careful not to come off as too brash, which can turn off your interviewer. Use the 8's confidence to pump yourself up.

If you feel secure during the interview, you may find it helpful to highlight the special skills and abilities you bring to the table by leaning into type 4. Without bashing other candidates, call out what your previous coworkers appreciated about you, as well as any certifications or expertise you will bring to the role.

As an Enneagram 2, your orientation to time is in the present, which will help you stay focused on making sure you're giving the interviewer what they need. Verbal processing may be a side effect of your orientation to time, so make sure you have prepared for the interview by diving deep into your STAR examples and have extracted only the most critical details to share. In stress, you may drift further into the future. Provide past examples of your work experience without getting too deep into hypothetical or ideal states. It's okay to talk about what you would do differently in future situations, but the bulk of what you're discussing should be what has already occurred and what the interviewer wants to discuss. If you're feeling secure in 4, it may be easier to be vulnerable about your previous experiences; however, be careful not to share too many negative feelings about past events.

Try to notice if you start to make yourself seem physically smaller in an interview, either by crossing your legs and arms or slouching, especially when talking about collaborating with a team. Sit up straight and lean forward, remaining engaged with the interviewer. Don't be afraid to take up an appropriate amount of space.

Questions to Ask the Interviewer

"Who should I connect with first to build relationships quickly?"

Finding the right people with whom to network and build relationships will set you up for success in your role. Your hiring manager will have good insight into who will be a great mentor, partner, stakeholder, or customer to get to know and work closely with. You'll want to identify the right people who can champion and support you as much as you will them.

"How much time am I expected to spend working on my own projects versus helping other members of the team?"

This question reveals that you enjoy supporting the people around you. If there are no opportunities to work closely with and support others on your team, this may not be the right fit. Note if the responses you get make it sound like you'll be holding too many hands and will have a hard time getting your own work done, you may find it challenging to set the right work-life balance for yourself in this job.

"What is something I could do to stand out in this role?"

You naturally want to find ways to make yourself indispensable, though not untenably so. This question shows you value high performance. Consider whether the interviewer's response aligns with how you would evaluate performance for this role. If there's time, parlay this into a longer conversation about performance reviews, so you know what to expect.

Support roles might come naturally to an Enneagram 2. Industries and roles to consider include Account Management, Executive Assistant, Recruiting, Fundraising, Hospitality, Event Planning, and Customer Service.

Reflection Questions

1. How can you make sure you are talking about your specific contributions in your STAR interview responses? Examine each of your examples and ensure you are discussing your own work. Don't worry, you're not bragging!

2. Does this role incorporate opportunities for you to grow your network and build relationships, or is it an isolated individual contributor position? If the latter, ask yourself if you could be successful in this role and find satisfaction in your work. Perhaps you are directly helping customers instead, which may satisfy this need.
3. How can you set yourself and your organization up for success in your next role, so you don't become the lone person everyone relies on? Being able to document, delegate, and plan for future succession is a sign of maturity.

Hiring Managers: Asking the Interview Questions

"Sorry, but I'm on the fence about this candidate," the hiring manager said, looking around the room for agreement and validation. At my large tech company, we were not allowed to be "on the fence," and for good reason: It typically meant you shouldn't be inclined to hire the candidate, but you wanted to give them a chance. Maybe you liked them as a person or felt bad for rejecting them. If that was the case, it was clear they were not the perfect match for the role and would be unlikely to succeed.

We went around the room sharing evaluations, which were mixed. Half of the room was interested in hiring the candidate, while the other half was against it. The hiring manager was in the middle, and she didn't want to budge.

She refused to commit to one side or the other for the entire debrief, and we determined the candidate would not be a fit. Afterwards, I hung around to talk to the hiring manager about why she couldn't decide.

"Honestly, I think it's mean; this person might be okay in the role, and I really liked them. Maybe they weren't strong in the values I was assessing, but they obviously were in others. I also have a track record of being 'not inclined', and I'm trying to be more open to group feedback."

She had effectively abandoned her own discernment to go along with the group, be liked, support the candidate, and expedite the process. The problem was this wasn't helpful for the company or the candidate.

Enneagram 2s may have a hard time judging candidates if they perceive them as trying their best, working hard, and having helpful traits. If they click with the candidate's personality, they may "rescue" the candidate during the interview by asking leading questions, giving them the answers, or even bending their own needs for the role to try to fit the candidate's strengths. On the other hand, they may be more critical of a candidate who doesn't demonstrate much emotional intelligence during an interview or who seems to be less of a team player.

An Enneagram 2 wants to forge a strong connection with a candidate. This can be a great strategy for helping the candidate feel comfortable and open, but it can lead to less honesty with the group in the final decision-making process. They may be concerned the candidate could feel led on when they are rejected.

Depending on how much time they've had to craft a narrative, 2s may struggle with being vulnerable, which influences the candidate they're interviewing to be guarded as well. As a result, answers may come off as performative rather than authentic connection points.

It can be more difficult for a 2 to remember to identify a candidate's specific accomplishments in each example. They should pay close attention to "I" statements and ensure the candidate is showing off their own skills outside of their team.

Subtypes

Let's consider how subtypes can impact your performance in an interview. If you don't know your subtype, consider which of these three options resonates most with your experiences.

Self-preservation 2s may be the friendliest interviewers, providing the best candidate experience. They may not come off as authoritative, but they are able to gather more information than other types thanks to how quickly they can make connections.

Social 2s are good at selling a position to a candidate, creating a warm and open environment while presenting themselves as a leader. This is especially helpful if the social 2 is the hiring manager, who will ultimately be working with the hired candidate.

The one-to-one Enneagram 2s may accidentally get woefully underqualified candidates excited for the opportunity to work with them. They may have a more difficult time "letting go" in a debrief if others don't like the candidate as much as they do. They should do their best to remain objective and lean on others in the interview process to keep them grounded.

If you're a 2, tap into your 1 wing when it's time to review your notes after the interview. You need to hold yourself to an objective decision about whether the candidate is the best fit, no matter how you personally feel about them or what you feel you owe them out of kindness.

Tap into your 3 wing during the interview itself to come across as a leader. Own your and your team's accomplishments and demonstrate why they should be excited to join your team. This can help give you a confidence boost if you ever feel like you're talking to someone with more experience than you or who may doubt your competence or authority.

If you go to type 8 in stress during the interview, use your passion to talk about why you love your work, your team, and your organization. Try not to scare off the candidate by being too interrogative or intense with your questions.

If you're feeling secure, you may start feeling more like a type 4 during the interview, which is helpful for selling the role to a solid candidate who may have offers from other companies. Don't misrepresent the role while differentiating it from other opportunities.

Your orientation to time in the present means you are good at focusing on the conversation you're having with the candidate in the moment, making sure their needs are met and they are having a good experience. If you are stressed and not feeling good about the candidate, you might start thinking ahead about what you need to do later or how you're planning on talking to the recruiter about improving the pipeline of candidates moving forward. The job-seeker across the table from you requires your attention to have a good perception of your organization, so remain focused on the interview itself and save any follow-up for when you're working on your notes. If you're feeling secure in 4, you may accidentally launch into a long story about a similar experience from your team, which can take up too much time. Similarly, you might become too focused on one past example the candidate chooses to share. Ensure you're fully evaluating the candidate by balancing the past, present, and future in the interview: Keep an eye on the time and talk through three different interview questions.

While it can be helpful for selling the role, don't worry too much about how you are presenting yourself to the candidate. Due to the high-pressure environment, they're much more focused on the impression they're making on you, so they may not remember much beyond the basic feeling you left behind.

Interviewing Other Types

Become comfortable with pushing candidates to talk about their own achievements; if you find yourself interviewing a 2, you are likely to fall into the trap of not being able to tell what their contributions were. It's not a great sign if a candidate made themselves a process bottleneck in their previous role—they are probably qualified, but they won't set up the team, the company, or themselves for long-term success.

You may find you harmonize with a 9, as you both avoid conflict and prioritize keeping relationships smooth. It may be helpful to have a 9 on your team to help you boost morale, reduce conflict, and balance stronger personalities.

If you are both passionate about the same subjects, you might click with an 8 in an interview, especially if you're feeling a little bit nervous. Don't let what you have in common take over the interview; instead, use it to generate a deeper connection and gather more relevant information. An 8 might add some firepower to your team, and you can feel confident delegating to them when you are feeling overwhelmed with work.

Check any biases you have against Enneagram 3s, who may rub you the wrong way by presenting as too individualistic. Instead, find commonalities in achievement; a 3 may turn out to be another team member you can confidently delegate to.

Reflection Questions

1. Do you ever feel like you're giving candidates hints during an interview? Treat candidates kindly while pressing them for the information you're looking for. Don't help them or ask leading questions, especially if you know you are already leaning toward hiring them.
2. Are you overly concerned about a candidate's impression of you after being rejected? Turning down a candidate who's not a fit doesn't make you a bad person. Objectively consider the facts and make the right decision for the candidate and the organization.
3. Are you leading the interview or letting the candidate take the lead? Own your strength of creating a welcoming and safe environment for the candidate but keep them on track during the interview (look at the clock, nudge them if required, and grade them against an objective rubric).

CHAPTER 7

Enneagram 3 – The Achiever

"Be so good they can't ignore you."

—Steve Martin

I WAS FEELING confused as I reviewed my notes from a recent interview. We were looking for a mid-level designer; the candidate had listed achievement after achievement and even had a glowing reference from someone in the interview loop, yet I was not inclined to hire them.

I was still relatively new at interviewing, but I was used to nervous candidates relying on me to draw information out of them. In this case, however, I barely had time to ask clarifying questions; the candidate had a complete narrative at the ready for each question I asked. I knew the loop would be mostly inclined to hire them, so I had to be clear about why I didn't believe they were a good fit.

At our large tech company, we were expected to back up every decision with evidence and data. As I read my notes, I suddenly realized what was missing: mistakes, flaws, nervousness. Basically, everything that makes a candidate feel human. No one feels comfortable with vulnerability, but showing at least a little bit demonstrates grounded maturity.

Which is more compelling: talking about your glowing achievements or about all the challenges you faced while achieving them? I'd take the latter any day; that's how you get a good sense of a candidate's true capabilities.

In the end, I couldn't make a good enough case against that candidate. They were probably successful, but I made a note to watch out for this achievement-based disguise in the future. As a 6, I go to 3 in stress, which means if I'm impressed or intimidated by a candidate, I'm likely to eat their list of achievements right up. I had to get more comfortable pushing candidates to go deeper into the weeds with me.

Enneagram 3s are arguably the most prepared for the interview setting, as they tend to spend the most time thinking about how others perceive them. Their resumes are packed with impressive jobs and accomplishments, they have their STAR stories ready to go (complete with exceeded expectations), and they go into the interview already confident they're the best fit for the role.

If a 3 is interviewing for a job they might not be 100 percent qualified for, they may feel like they are on shaky ground. Similarly, if they are not "winning" their interviews, they may lose faith in themselves. They should beware of getting too caught up in what others think. Their success in life is not defined by their job or achievements.

If you are an Enneagram 3, to help soothe your nerves and improve your mindset, use these exercises:

1. Practice something you don't think you're "good" at. Do you have an interest you've always wanted to pursue but haven't because you're worried you might "fail"? This could be anything from watercolor painting to tennis to playing in a band. Challenge yourself to practice it weekly and pay attention to the process, not just the results. Learn to enjoy it

without performing perfectly, and this skill will translate to other aspects of your life.

2. Be open to conversation that doesn't fit your narrative. I challenge Enneagram 3s to think of presenting themselves beyond their accomplishments in an interview— both job-seekers and hiring managers. Consider addressing difficulties that have come up in your work, academic, or personal life (if appropriate). Talk about your hobbies. Laugh off your mistakes and show your personal growth. You may not believe me, but I promise you don't have to be flawless in an interview setting; you already deserve to be in the room, and you can show up as your full, sometimes messy, human self. This will create a bond that could end up being the foundation of your future working relationship. If you need more self-reflection, take some time to journal or check in with yourself to help you feel comfortable with all your different parts (you may find it helpful to make this an ongoing daily practice).

Job-Seekers: Responding to Interview Questions

The candidate smiled ear to ear as she waited for my next interview question. Looking polished with a trendy custom-tailored suit, a perfectly smooth bob, and flawless makeup, she was one of the most prepared candidates I had ever spoken to. She had just finished telling me about her greatest professional accomplishment, and indeed, it was impressive.

It was a global company-wide program that required a great deal of organization, reporting, collaboration, and problem-solving. The data she brought to the interview proved her impact on both her customer and the company. I was looking forward to hearing more about the challenges: What had she struggled with? What did she learn from the experience? This is my favorite part of hearing about a program of this scope, as I've led similar initiatives that included many blunders and bumps along the way.

"Can you tell me what you would do differently, if you could go back and do it again?"

She paused, thinking about her response, and I noticed a little panic creeping into her eyes. Still, her smile remained.

"No, there's nothing I would do differently."

"Really? Surely, in a project of this scope, there's at least one small thing you would change."

She shook her head and doubled down. "I know it sounds too good to be true, but it's my greatest professional accomplishment because it was perfect."

"Okay, no problem," I pivoted. "Can you give me an example of a different large project where you made a mistake?"

She bit her lip and wracked her brain. "Honestly, not since I was a junior PM. Sorry." By now, she seemed almost confused that I kept probing for faults. Shouldn't I be impressed at how great she was at her job and leave it at that?

While it was great the candidate had examples ready to go and specific evidence of the impact of her work, I was concerned she didn't have any examples of mistakes, learning, or growth. Maybe she didn't feel comfortable revealing too much in the interview. Unfortunately, this was a consistent issue in all six of her interviews, so we could never be sure how she would handle setbacks in the workplace—which meant we couldn't risk hiring her for the role.

Often, 3s do not understand the value of this kind of human connection in an interview setting. She was probably ready for "Tell me about your weaknesses," as many candidates prepare for this question. I suspect she would have said, "I'm too much of a perfectionist," the classic nonanswer.

Let's dig a little deeper into how Enneagram 3s may want to tailor their interview preparation.

Question that may be easy to answer:

"Can you tell me about your greatest professional achievement?"

Like in the example I just shared, answering this question might come naturally to you as a 3; you probably have a few different ideas of what you want to share, plus the data to back it up. When you give your example, you want to reflect on what was challenging for you about the project. Consider the question from a place of humility: What could you have done better? Trust me, there's always something, and you will come off as much more self-aware if you're able to call it out and talk about how you'll address that in future projects or processes.

Question that may be more difficult to answer:

"Can you tell me about a time you made a mistake and had to enlist someone else's help to solve the problem?"

If you're an Enneagram 3, you may like to solve problems yourself. That's not because you're a martyr or you want people to like you (like a 2), but you want to look good and get the dopamine hit of crossing more achievements off your list. You may think it's a sign of weakness to ask for help, so you may grind yourself to the bone to avoid it. That's why you'll really stand out in an interview if you have an answer to this question at the ready.

You may feel more comfortable answering this question with an example where you had to work with an expert in an area unrelated to your field. For example, as a PM, I often reached out to business analysts who understood SQL tables much better than I did. Alternatively, you may have an example of a time when you wanted to set better boundaries at work, so you asked your manager to help you prioritize tasks. As much as you value your independence, being able to prove you can ask for help when needed will show the interviewer you aren't a burnout risk.

Subtypes

Let's consider how subtypes can impact your performance in an interview. If you don't know your subtype, consider which of these three options resonates most with your experiences.

Self-preservation 3s would rather demonstrate their fit for the role through their exceptional performance rather than talk themselves up in an interview. They may even slip into self-deprecation because they don't want to show off. Self-preservation 3s should instead proudly share all they've accomplished in their career, without being too modest, to feel firmly in the driver's seat. They may need to actively work on showing weakness to click with someone in an interview.

Social 3s may like interviewing and may be used to easily impressing others. Whether they flex their fancy degrees and work accomplishments or show up wearing their best suit and a Rolex, they want to be aspirational. They expect to "win" the interview, so rejection may come as a surprise to them. That said, they probably already have a backup plan, which is helpful. They should try not to focus too much on prestige or money during the interview process (though they should negotiate when the time finally comes to accept an offer).

The one-to-one Enneagram 3s may find they fall into gendered societal conditioning, and so they show up how they are "supposed to." Traditionally, this may mean masculine 3s come off as more assertive or ambitious, while feminine 3s are quieter and humbler. Either way, their focus may be on pleasing the interviewer. These 3s may talk more about successful results of a project based on good reviews from other team members or stakeholders, rather than on hard data or personal satisfaction. They may struggle with providing honest examples of failure; to overcome this, they should practice being vulnerable with a friend or a partner before an interview.

If you're a 3, tap into your 2 wing by demonstrating how your efforts helped other team members or your manager in the past. Examples of times you took ownership of a project outside your scope or helped unburden others on the team who were struggling can show how you form sturdy relationships with coworkers.

Differentiate from other candidates by tapping into your 4 wing. Show off what makes you unique or special or discuss a quality you bring that other candidates may not have. Are you a subject-matter expert in a highly sought-after skill? Make sure one of the STAR examples you prepare will highlight that.

In stress, you go into 9, so beware of being stumped by a question and trying to avoid it. Rather than deflecting, think of the closest appropriate example, even if it's a little bit of a stretch. As discussed earlier, this may come up most often when you're asked about mistakes or faults. While you want to avoid overpreparation, you should have one of these examples in your back pocket before the interview.

If you're feeling especially confident, you may get ahead of yourself by leaning into 6 and trying to answer any potential follow-up questions in advance. Share the pertinent details, but don't try to stump your interviewer.

Enneagram 3s like to focus on the future, so if you're not careful, you may get caught up in providing hypothetical or ideal answers, rather than referencing situations based on fact. On the bright side, you will ace any questions about where you want to be in five years.

When you're stressed in 9, your orientation to time can shift to the past. If you get too in your head, you may get stuck thinking about a situation where you weren't happy with your performance, to the point where you have a hard time coming up with the best example. If you learned from that experience and can speak to what you'd do differently, I challenge you to go ahead and share the first example that comes to mind. Vulnerability will help you come off as more human to your interviewer.

If you're feeling confident, you may find it easier to stay in the present in 6. Just try not to let surprises (like accidentally saying the wrong word, a yawn from the interviewer, or a fire alarm going off) distract you from the task at hand.

Don't memorize your answers to interview questions, don't try to control your body language, and don't hold yourself to unrealistic expectations. Feel a tickle in your throat? Take a sip of water and move on. If you feel your responses are getting away from you or moving in a different direction than expected, keep smiling and let the conversation progress naturally.

Questions to Ask the Interviewer

"What are the team's biggest current challenges?"

Why would you ask this question? You want to be the one to solve the problem, of course! This will likely exceed your hiring manager's expectations for what you can reasonably tackle when you start, and if you're able to fully understand this challenge and get to work on it once you're in the role, you will see great dividends. This question also demonstrates that you are a problem solver: You don't care solely about achieving your own goals but about solving problems for customers and your team.

"What goals would I be expected to meet or exceed in order to be successful this year?"

This question shows how seriously you'll take your job, which will result in a smoother onboarding process. You can decide, based on how they answer this question, if the role is right for you. Maybe you're a good salesperson, but you don't want more than 50 percent of your salary to be commission-based, or you don't want external market factors to potentially impede your professional growth. In short, expectations go both ways, and you want everyone to be happy.

"What opportunities are there for growth and professional development within the company?"

If you are a 3, you're probably used to exceeding expectations and being promoted quickly. This question will help you understand if that's possible for you within this organization. At a senior level, you may find ceilings quicker at smaller organizations. Within larger companies, you may find more chances for lateral moves that keep you fulfilled and create growth opportunities. Beware of saying yes to a company where promotion is limited, as you will be looking for another job sooner than you might expect.

Industries and roles to consider as a 3 include anything business-related: Finance, Sales, Marketing, and the like all tend to be a great fit. Real Estate and Entertainment are other industries where achievement-focused people shine. Leadership roles, including executive and founder roles, come naturally to a 3. Being a Lawyer, Politician, or other type of Performer or Influencer may feel rewarding as well, if they are able to be successful.

Reflection Questions

1. Thinking beyond your accomplishments, how else do you want to show up in the interview? What are the messy parts of your career you think are valuable to share? Who are you when you're not at work? What are your first principles in life?
2. Have you been memorizing responses as you prepare for interviews? Try practicing with a friend and ask them if you are coming across as more human or robotic.
3. Do you really want this role, or do you just want the title or company as the next step on your resume? Choose a position that will provide personal satisfaction, not just social status.

Hiring Managers: Asking the Interview Questions

"Are we sure the person who fills this role needs a graduate degree?" I asked gently. We were all tired; it was 4:49 p.m. on a Thursday, and the other interview loop participants were all looking at the clock, willing the minutes to go by faster.

"Of course, it's always been in the job description," the hiring manager insisted.

"Right, but all the candidates have either been MBAs straight out of school or senior levels without a degree who have the other qualifications you're looking for. Finding a mid-level MBA has been challenging, and I think we've passed up some great candidates along the way."

The hiring manager had been hired as a young MBA himself, and he had accrued several years of experience and many internal successes since then. He had been with the company for so long he couldn't remember just how inexperienced fresh MBA graduates were.

"Plenty of people have both a graduate degree and career experience," he spat from across the table.

"Yes," I explained, "but we wouldn't be hiring those people at this level; we'd be offering them jobs at the next level up. Your level."

I found it confusing that MBAs automatically came into our company at the same level many people retired at. It was hard to compare where candidates landed on the spectrum of "book smarts" versus professional experience, and determine how they would be able to perform within the company based on that assessment.

I continued, "I don't have a graduate degree. But I'm currently raising the bar at this level, and I could arguably do this job myself."

The hiring manager nodded, sizing me up. We had experience working together cross- functionally on a few projects, so he knew I wasn't bluffing.

"Maybe I'd make an exception for you. Do you want to switch teams?" he joked, knowing he was accountable for this lengthy candidate search.

"How about we come up with a list of your true non-negotiables?" I said, "Let's focus on functional skills and values instead of shiny accomplishments."

The hiring manager agreed. He and the recruiter aligned on the dealbreakers for the role and set realistic expectations for finding candidates. In the end, he was so focused on his own achievements and looking good to others that he simply didn't understand why someone wouldn't have a graduate degree, a big award, and a resume full of accomplishments by the time they're 24 years old— a stereotypical Enneagram 3.

There's plenty of time to become successful in life, but in an interview, you need to be able to assess the factors you won't be able to train into a candidate. These include soft skills like customer service or dealing with conflict, which MBA candidates often haven't had much exposure to. That's why I look for experience over degrees.

Let's talk about how some of an Enneagram 3's tendencies can get in the way of interviewing and hiring.

Have you ever wondered about a candidate's first impression of you during an interview? Maybe you didn't consciously realize it, but you still shared your own career accomplishments when introducing yourself and took up too much time talking about your team's recent wins. There's always a power dynamic at play within an interview, but you don't want to make the candidate feel even more inferior. If the candidate isn't providing the detailed information you're looking for, they may be nervous about showing any weakness, especially when asked about their mistakes. To ease the tension, share a casual (and professional) example of one of your own past blunders.

If the candidate has not met or exceeded your expectations within the first 15 minutes of the interview, you may feel like they're wasting your time. Rather than stewing across the table, give this person a chance. Maybe they're just warming up. Perhaps they haven't met your standards yet, but they still could—while working on your team. Even if it turns out the candidate isn't a fit, every "bad" interview gets you one step closer to the right hire. Regardless, every candidate you speak to deserves your respect and attention in exchange for their time.

Be careful if you're interviewing someone close to your own level, as you may find yourself "competing" with them—either out loud or in your head. Turn this around and use your competitive drive for good. They may be better than you at some things, but won't that ensure your team's future success? I had a great director who always strove to hire people he thought could surpass him (and maybe even fire him) someday. Working closely with someone who challenges you will make you even sharper.

Subtypes

Let's consider how subtypes can impact your performance in an interview. If you don't know your subtype, consider which of these three options resonates most with your experiences.

Self-preservation 3s may feel too responsible for the interview loop and assert too much power. They should make sure they are collaborating with the recruiters (and everyone else in the loop) to make the right decisions. They should aim to display more vulnerability during an interview to help the candidate come out of their shell more, which will enable them to see the candidate as a full human rather than just their resume.

Social 3s need to be the most careful about getting too competitive with a candidate close to their skill level or talking too much about their own achievements. They will do a lot to create a positive experience for the candidate, so they think highly of them, but they struggle with showing any weakness. To truly connect, they should show they aren't perfect.

The one-to-one Enneagram 3s need to be careful of going along with group mentality when hiring, especially if pleasing their superiors would mean voting against their gut. They should be wary of looking at each candidate as the potential perfect hire, as they will be disappointed (even with a great hire) when they discover that person's faults. Candidates love interacting with them, so one-to-ones should try to stay as objective and data-oriented as possible.

As a 3, lean into your 2 wing by taking care of the candidate during the interview, making sure they get water and bathroom breaks.

Trade your discomfort for genuine connection by sharing one of your difficult experiences or mistakes to earn their trust.

Look for special qualities in each candidate by using your 4 wing. Sell the position to them by showing they can be themselves and be accepted. Talk to them about how they would be a good fit for the team and how they could stand out.

In stress, you go to 9, so be careful not to stall out in the middle of the interview or feel like you're on a sinking ship if it feels like a waste of time. Don't back away from asking the tough questions so as not to rock the boat; keep asking them (kindly), even if it's awkward. You may be judging too early.

If you're feeling confident, you may find yourself playing devil's advocate with the candidate in 6, coming up with some impressive (and challenging!) follow-up questions. This can come off as intense or discouraging to candidates, so try to keep the conversation as positive and enjoyable as you can.

If you're an Enneagram 3, your orientation to time in the future may cause you to start daydreaming about how a promising candidate will perform in the role—or how they might fall short. Keep yourself in the present moment by checking in with your senses: What do you see and hear in front of you? Save your judgment for after the interview.

If you're stressed in 9 and you're not enjoying yourself, you might start comparing the candidate to previous employees you've hired or let go. Again, keep yourself in the present to ensure you're asking the right questions. If you're confident and enjoying the conversation, you will find it much easier to be an active listener.

Your body language should show you are open to authentic connection by leaning back in your seat a little. As someone who is naturally ambitious, this may help you come across as more relatable or relaxed.

Interviewing Other Types

When interviewing another 3, you may become especially competitive as you each try to one-up each other. You may not notice you're doing it at first, but if you catch yourself in the act, try to use it as an opportunity to bond with them. Either way, let the candidate have the spotlight.

When interviewing someone you suspect is a 2, you may be drawn into your shared desire to make other people like you. You may see the 2 as someone who can take care of the rest of your team while you're off conquering meetings or projects. They could become your right-hand person someday.

Type 1s are appealing during an interview because they're direct and improvement- oriented, so they usually come prepared with examples of helping their past teams become even better. They are driven by doing the "right" thing, so you may bond over ethics or compliance as well. They're great people to have on your team to ensure quality pairs with your focus on action and accomplishment.

If a candidate is "too forward" about past mistakes or failures, do your best to not build up a bias against them, as they may be an 8 who could be a great powerhouse for your team.

Have you ever interviewed someone who seemed too relaxed? This is often the case with a 7; they are calm and go with the flow, knowing they will get the role if it's the right fit for them. You may find them too positive, carefree, or informal, but if you can determine they're capable of exceeding expectations, they may be a great choice to even out your team dynamic and make you all more productive and less stressed.

I can't say this enough for 3s: Give every candidate a chance, even up to the last minute of the interview, you truly never know what you're going to get.

Reflection Questions

1. Can you look beyond the candidate's shiny exterior and dig into the messier parts of their responses? It's great if they meet your career expectations, but they need to demonstrate resilience and growth.
2. When was the last time you shared a mistake with anyone? Have you ever done it during an interview? If you come off as extremely polished yourself, you may want to encourage the candidate to trust you by sharing one of your less-than-perfect moments.
3. Are you and your interview loop aligned on must-haves for the role, and are they realistic given the current job market and pool of candidates available? If hiring for a role takes longer than three months and you have a steady stream of candidates, take a closer look at your expectations as a group to determine if they are realistic and appropriate.

CHAPTER 8

Enneagram 4 – The Individualist

"To be yourself in a world that is constantly trying to make you something else is the greatest accomplishment."

—Ralph Waldo Emerson

ON MY FIRST day stepping into my "real" job after college—an associate producer at a digital agency—I remember my manager walking me around to introduce me to everyone working at their desks. No one was interested in meeting the new girl; even my future husband barely looked at me before he turned back to his work. One designer thought my boss was joking: I must have been her niece, not the new associate producer, because I looked so out of place. In the end, being paraded around the office left me confused and a little embarrassed.

I did not fit the typical demographic of the agency. I was younger, I proudly told everyone I had been in a sorority, and I put too much effort into my outfits for such a casual workplace. Meanwhile, most of my coworkers were at least five years older than me and were proudly counterculture, were often HR-inappropriate, and liked to hang out at the nearby bars after work.

I knew I wanted to be myself, but that version of me wasn't going to fit in easily here. I had two choices: I could stay frustrated about being different and try to blend in, or I could be myself and focus on doing my best work. I chose the latter: I put my head down, worked hard, built relationships, and tried to show everyone else I deserved to be there. I embraced my differences and continued to show up as myself. In time, I was accepted; my coworkers recognized the value of my work and considered me a peer.

While I've probably worked with a lot of non-conforming 4s, this was the professional experience where I felt most like a 4 myself. Today, I'm grateful the senior managers saw my potential beyond my trying-too-hard exterior and could tell I would be successful at the company.

The difference between me and an Enneagram 4 is that the latter are often looking for opportunities to break free from the crowd and show off their unique, authentic selves. Whereas I wished I could blend in, a 4 in this scenario may have relished the opportunity to stand out. Interviews can be the perfect place to differentiate from others and show up proudly—or be misunderstood. If you're a 4 getting ready for an interview, your mindset and the way you frame the experience may make all the difference.

On the day of the interview or in preparation, make room for these activities:

1. Settle your nerves by creating a pre-interview ritual for yourself. It could be taking a bath the evening before, setting an intention for how you want to show up, eating your favorite meal, or grabbing your preferred coffee drink on the way to the interview. Mindfully construct a ritual you can repeat for future interviews and reward yourself for a job well done.

2. Consider your unique perspective on the push-pull of standing out versus being part of a team. Are you interviewing for a position where you'll need to be able to collaborate closely with others? Make sure you have STAR examples to demonstrate that skill, especially with initial conflict you had to work through. If you're the interviewer, are you concerned about a potential bias from other interviewers on the loop? Think about how you can get the right data from the candidate to counteract group think. Show the candidate they are free to be themselves.

Job-Seekers: Responding to Interview Questions

I've worked with a lot of designers in my career and would not be surprised if many of them typed themselves as Enneagram 4. They're extremely creative, bold, and expressive, and I love working with these folks. I once had a job where I interviewed many designers, and I always looked forward to reviewing their portfolios. Even if we didn't end up hiring someone, I saw how skilled they were in their craft, and I appreciated their hard work.

There was one portfolio review our team was eager about. What we had seen from the candidate was extremely promising, and they seemed to be a perfect fit with our personalities as well. The interview started out well enough, but then I caught the eye of one of my peers, who subtly gestured under the table for me to look— I hadn't noticed the candidate had taken off their shoes. That was certainly unusual.

In my best impression of Bill Hader's character Stefon from Saturday Night Live, the portfolio review had everything: bare feet, a physical product design unrelated to our work, dramatic stories, and even a tearful outburst. We left the portfolio review unsure of what our future one-on-one interviews would hold. Sometimes a rocky start leads to a surprising result— or at the very least, a great story.

After his one-on-one later that day, my manager walked into our shared office. I searched his face for any hint of what to expect from my interview. Always professional, he simply smiled and said, "They're a designer, all right."

Taking that as a positive sign, I walked into my one-on-one interview looking forward to the conversation. It was clear the candidate felt comfortable in the interview setting; they were relaxed. I love easy-flowing conversation, and thankfully, it started out well. I quickly learned, however, there is such a thing as being too comfortable.

"Can you tell me about your favorite and least favorite managers?" I asked.

"For sure!" The candidate perked up. "There was one manager I loved to work with. She was smoking hot!"

I blinked in disbelief. The candidate didn't seem to notice; they continued to talk about the manager's attractiveness, like it was her best quality. I asked for a more professional reason why she was a good manager, with minimal results. The candidate also said their least favorite manager was British, and they didn't like British people. Again, I asked if there was a more professional reason for their dislike, and they said no.

Throughout the interview, the candidate kept using inappropriate examples and even profanity. To this day, I'm not sure why they felt their behavior would get them the job, but I suspect they felt comfortable with us and wanted to stand out. This is an extreme example, of course; I'm sure you know better than to commit HR violations for the sake of "being authentic."

Let's discuss better strategies for differentiating yourself from other candidates to make a strong impression in an interview.

Question that may be easy to answer:

"Can you tell me about a particular work-related setback you have faced?"

One of the hard parts about being a 4 is it's easy to slip into a victim's mindset. If you're a 4, this question may seem challenging at first; however, it's an opportunity to reframe and demonstrate how you handle setbacks. It's okay to prepare an example you have a strong reaction to. In fact, that may strengthen your answer. The key is making sure you don't stay in the doldrums when describing your experience; don't choose an example that brings you to tears or you haven't fully processed. Think of a time when you had an initially negative reaction, then shifted it into a positive result.

Question that may be more difficult to answer:

"Can you tell me about a business situation when you felt honesty would be inappropriate?"

To be fair, this is a very tricky behavioral interview question for any type, and not one I would recommend employers use. With that said, 4s may be especially challenged by this one - they rarely feel honesty is inappropriate. I recommend answering honestly that you value integrity, then giving an example demonstrating you can be direct without being too harsh.

Subtypes

Let's consider how subtypes can impact your performance in an interview. If you don't know your subtype, consider which of these three options resonates most with your experiences.

Self-preservation 4s are likely to come across as appealing to interviewers, as they have great examples of toughing out difficult situations and working hard toward a goal. They should ask enough questions to know if a role is a good fit for them, rather than making a quick decision to leave their job for a shiny new one without fully understanding what they're getting into.

Social 4s need to be careful not to bring too much negativity from past roles or coworkers into the interview. They may have a harder time talking themselves up or providing examples impressive enough for the interviewer. They should resist the urge to compare themselves with other candidates, interviewers, or past coworkers; instead, they should focus on their own achievements.

The one-to-one Enneagram 4s may have a hard time waiting after an interview to hear if they got the job, as they assume they are the best person for the role. During the interview, if they feel they aren't impressing the interviewer enough, they should try not to show frustration, which might hurt their chances.

If you're a 4, pull out your long list of accomplishments and hard work to tap into your 3 wing. You won't have as much trouble as other types with preparing STAR responses to interview questions.

Ahead of the interview, do your research and make sure you know about the role, the company, and the potential interviewers you will be meeting with. These strengths from your 5 wing will support your ability to show up professionally and differentiate yourself from other candidates.

Enneagram 4s go to 2 in stress, do not make any concessions and continue to advocate for your own needs. Share examples where you helped others or formed a valuable connection in the workplace. Focus on building a relationship with the person interviewing you.

If you're feeling secure during the interview, you'll come off more like a decisive 1, which could give you a confidence boost. Be careful not to seem too rigid but do assertively show off your subject-matter expertise.

Your orientation to time is the past, which means it's probably easy for you to immerse yourself in previous experiences and turn them into great stories for the interviewer. Give yourself a little bit of distance so you don't get too caught up in the riptide of feelings you may have about past events. If you're stressed and feeling more like a 2, you may find it easier to be in the present moment but be careful of getting too caught up in worrying your answers are good enough. Trust yourself and the process. If you're feeling confident and more like a 1, you might find yourself answering questions with hypotheticals. If you suspect you're doing this, feel free to ask the interviewer if you're providing the responses they expect, and ground yourself in your real-life work examples.

Pay attention to whether your responses are flowing like a river or dripping like a leaky faucet. If the latter, you may be feeling withdrawn, which means you need to put in more effort to get the conversation flowing more freely. While others enjoy how passionate and focused you can be, they may not enjoy constant deep eye contact, so be sure to glance at your notes or around the room from time to time for variation.

Questions to Ask the Interviewer

"How would you describe the company's culture and values?"

To show up authentically, you'll want to assess how you would "fit into" the work environment. You might enjoy the opportunity to stand out as special and different, and you want to make sure the company will support you. You will want to confirm the company's values align with yours.

"What is the company's policy for how many outside-of-work functions employees are required to attend?"

You have hobbies and interests outside of work that you value. You're probably not the first in line at the bar every happy hour, and that's fine. But you do want to be sure it won't negatively impact your performance or career progression at the company.

"Do you have any reservations about my qualifications or experience?"

This is a sneaky way to gauge the temperament of the interviewer, but also a way to make sure you aren't misunderstood. If you disagree with their assessment, this isn't the time to argue, but you could say, "Oh! That surprises me. I guess I should have given you more examples about [insert more satisfying example of the qualification in question]." If there's still time left in the interview, you may get a shot at redemption here. Keep the conversation low-pressure, interesting, and in the interviewer's court.

Type 4s are often attracted to expression and connection, so they may be interested in roles related to Design, Creativity, Psychology, Branding, or Fashion. They want to leave their own mark on their work, company, or industry.

Reflection Questions

1. How do you stand out from the typical candidates for this role or from other employees at this company? What are your strongest assets you want to highlight in your next interview? If they relate to the job you're interviewing for (they should!), bring these to the forefront so you can shine!

2. How do your values, ethics, and expectations for organizational culture and communication align with this role? Ask dealbreaker questions during the interview. Make it clear that you won't be betraying yourself by taking the job.
3. Have you found yourself trapped in the limiting mindset that being different is the reason you haven't been getting the jobs you want? Don't let a long job-seeking journey get you down— you will find the right fit. Resist the urge to fit into a mold just to get a job (unless it's necessary and temporary).

Hiring Managers: Asking the Interview Questions

I once worked with a senior hiring manager who was struggling to articulate why she wasn't interested in hiring a certain designer, even though they checked all the boxes. She mentioned "culture fit," a typical indicator of trusting gut instinct over data.

"Do you think this candidate could perform the duties of this job and exceed expectations?" I asked patiently.

"Well, yes…"

"Did anything inappropriate happen during the interview, something that gave you HR-related concerns?"

"No!" She sounded exasperated as she struggled to explain how she felt.

Blindly trusting your intuition can be tricky for 4s because projection or mood can feel like a hunch. I asked the hiring manager to listen to our experiences with the candidate, and ultimately, she decided it was worth extending an offer to them.

A few months after the designer ramped up, the manager pulled me aside. "You all were right," she said. "We made a great hire decision; it's been going really well."

I asked her why she thought she'd had such an intense original reaction to the candidate, and she said, "I think it was a combination of difficult things going on in my personal life and the nervousness I was picking up from the candidate. It felt too good to be true, but it was all me. Thanks for being patient with me!"

When you feel so deeply, you may have a hard time separating your own feelings from others' or figuring out what those feelings are trying to tell you. All interviewers on the loop should fully understand the role and what you're looking for in a candidate so you don't feel misunderstood or like you're all wasting time. A single hiring process can take months, so you should consider if dwindling energy levels and stamina may be contaminating your discernment.

If you're hiring someone around your level, watch out for any feelings of insecurity or competition that may arise. If any candidates across as extremely unique, be wary, as connecting with a "kindred spirit" might cloud your judgment.

Subtypes

Let's consider how subtypes can impact your performance in an interview. If you don't know your subtype, consider which of these three options resonates most with your experiences.

Self-preservation 4s may feel discouraged or like a "cog in the machine" when stuck in a long hiring process. They may benefit from regrouping with their recruiter, an accountability buddy, or a mentor to reset and keep them aligned with their goals.

Social 4s should be careful not to be too negative about a candidate during an interview and the debrief afterward. They should try to find positive aspects in every candidate, even the ones who bomb their interview. It's easy to get too wrapped up in the drama of a long hiring process so it could be helpful to consider coming up with a reward for themselves when their hiring goal is achieved.

The one-to-one Enneagram 4s should reflect on their own interview experiences and how they want to contribute to the candidate's. For example, a 4 who's been put through bad interview experiences at their company may want to subject their interviewees to the same, but that would not get them closer to their end goal. They should tap into their desire for competition by always trying to hire the next best person for their team.

If interviews stress you out and you struggle with feeling like an impostor when you lead them, leaning into your 3 wing will help remind you that you deserve to be determining the fate of the candidate in front of you. Recall your accomplishments in your role and beyond and walk into the interview room with confidence.

Use your analytical 5 wing skills when evaluating a candidate after an interview. This can help separate your gut feelings from reality and allow you to show up to the debrief without a bias you may not have realized you have.

You go to 2 in stress. Think about the comfort level of the candidate you're talking to. Ask them if they need a break, make sure they're feeling psychologically safe, and show your warmth. It's hard to go through an interview loop; a friendly face can make all the difference.

Feeling secure in your interviewing skills? It will be clear to the candidate that you have high standards for quality, and you may start to come off as rigid. Make it clear with both your body language and your words that you are open to their responses, even if they are different than what you might expect.

An Enneagram 4's orientation to time is the past, so be careful not to let your mind wander to your own past situations like the candidate's;

you can reflect on this when you review your notes. If you're stressed and in 2, you may have an easier time staying in the present and focusing on the candidate's impression of you and your organization. This can be particularly useful if the interview is not going well but don't want them to leave with a bad taste in their mouth.

If interviewing with confidence, you might spend too much time thinking or talking about the future, with or without the candidate. Keep yourself focused on the conversation.

Tone down the intensity of your body language during an interview, especially if you're excited about the candidate. Alternatively, if you feel yourself retreating in your chair or giving the candidate very little to work with, it may be a sign you're not interested in them. Put more effort into the conversation to ensure you're making the most of your time together.

Interviewing Other Types

You might bond with another Enneagram 4 who's a "black sheep" like you or who's proud of being a subject-matter expert. Be sure to fall back on data when making your decision, as this is another case where you might be biased by "vibes."

You may click with type 5s, who are clear about their boundaries and need focused time at work. They tend to specialize and take a lot of pride in their work, so if you have a strong 5 wing, you might feel a natural bond forming.

You appreciate 9s who would rather go along with your vision and leadership than rock the boat. Having a solid member of your team who can help provide harmony and stability will lead to successful results. Type 9 candidates are likely to be especially impressed by the qualities that make you stand out in your job; it's always nice to be recognized!

Type 7s tend to like 4s, but it's not always a two-way street, so be careful if you notice yourself bristling during an interview with a candidate who seems too breezy for your taste. This person could bring some much-needed levity or charisma to your team, if you give them a chance. They are likely to want to impress you due to your "cool kid" vibe.

Candidates who are 8s might bother you if they trigger your fears of being "too much" by displaying what it can look like in a professional setting. Rather than giving in to this bias, consider how this person could lead the charge for your team by advocating for you or clearing roadblocks.

Reflection Questions

1. Is your hiring decision based on your notes or on "vibes"? Always come back to the facts.
2. Do you find yourself wanting to differentiate from the rest of the interview loop? Watch out for this; agreeing about a candidate is a good thing.
3. Have you ever suspected a candidate may be acting differently with you than with other interviewers? This may be the case, especially during a long day of interviews. In this high-pressure setting, people do not always show up exactly as they will in the job. If the data demonstrates this person can do the job, give them the chance to come to you more authentically on their first day of work and beyond.

CHAPTER 9

Enneagram 5 – The Investigator

"Somewhere, something incredible is waiting to be known."

—Carl Sagan

I HAVE A 5 wing, so when a topic interests me, I dive in headfirst, reading all the books and listening to all the podcasts I can find. I collect these "special interests" and all information associated with them with so much fervor, it's hard for me to imagine someone else might not feel the same way. My fascinations with psychology, herbalism, longevity, and my favorite podcasts, books, and television shows all take up a large part of my brain, which is then shared with my friends and family on a regular basis. I have received feedback from close friends several times about being perceived as a know-it-all when I thought I was just sharing information they would find interesting.

The times when I can connect with someone else over one of my shared interests feel like complete bliss to me. All my worries and even my surroundings seem to fade away when I'm lost in conversation. As someone who is very risk-averse, it's probably the most I let myself feel out of control. It's a meaningful form of intimacy for me.

Even though I'm aware sometimes this is not reciprocated, there are still times I will catch myself five sentences in and notice my friend or husband's glazed-over expression and pause. Aren't they as interested in this as I am? How long have I been ranting about this? Did I accidentally say something that could be misinterpreted? Oops! This is not how you want to feel in a professional setting.

If you're an Enneagram 5 and you are asked about a topic you're knowledgeable in or learning about, you may find yourself in this familiar predicament. Provide the level of detail the interviewer needs, but pay close attention to their cues and ensure you aren't so deep down a rabbit hole that you don't even remember the original question. Let's explore more of the specific difficulties 5s may face in an interview.

I have such a soft spot in my heart for Enneagram 5s. Interviews can be such a paradox for this type: exciting as it means learning more about a new company and role, but terrifying as it means interacting in a high-pressure one-on-one environment (and probably using up your energy for the day).

Getting ready for an interview includes creating space to give yourself what you need, protecting your energy, and resisting the urge to memorize answers to potential interview questions.

On the day of the interview or during prep make room for a couple of activities:

1. Ground yourself. Do you already know the best way to center yourself, or do you need to explore this more? For some people, it's meditating, napping, enjoying their favorite coffee or tea, doing yoga, touching their feet to the earth or a body of water, or gardening. Chances are high you need to be by yourself to feel fully grounded and in touch with your body,

mind, and spirit. Carve out time leading up to the interview to calm your nerves and recharge. Type 5s can be especially sensitive to rejection, so if you're a job-seeker who has not been called back after an interview, take a moment to release any grief or shame you feel about recent experiences so those feelings don't follow you into the next interview. You can journal to process the feelings, write them on scrap paper and burn them, or visualize them leaving your body through your feet and into the ground.

2. Do your research. Instead of trying to memorize responses to specific interview questions, identify a couple of examples from past jobs that relate to the position you are interviewing for. Once it's done, trust you will be able to answer questions well in the moment and turn your excited mind to researching other aspects of the company, interviewer, or role. What don't you already know that you're excited to learn about? Make a short list and craft the questions you'll ask your interviewer. Did you find something you and the interviewer have in common? Ask them a question about it. Use your best judgment as to what is appropriate to bring up, as the interviewer may be unsettled by the thought that you may have thoroughly googled them beforehand.

Job-Seekers: Responding to Interview Questions

I have interviewed many economists who I suspect were Enneagram 5s: extremely knowledgeable about their specific area of study for their PhD. A junior economist I was working with was inspired by the interview question I asked her and quickly dove into a rabbit hole of context about her job market paper. I was grateful for the background, as I was a PM by trade and did not have the same background in her industry, but the clock was ticking, and I wasn't getting the information I required to determine if she would be successful in the role and the company.

In this case, I had to gently interrupt her a few times to get the interview back on track. I ended up asking her fewer questions than usual, and while the conversation did flow, she did most of the talking. I could tell she had a lot to offer, but nothing she said related to the role she was interviewing for. Quite a bit of effort went into teasing out her functional skills and how she built relationships.

On the other side of the coin, I've conducted interviews where I spent almost half the time trying to ask the right questions so the candidate felt comfortable providing the details I requested. I've interviewed plenty of folks who struck me as 5s once I got to know them, but it took extra effort to get them to trust me enough to open up.

Whether you resonate with oversharing or clamming up, making the best use of your time in an interview is one of the main areas of focus for a 5.

Question that may be easy to answer:

"Can you tell me about a time you had to dive deep to solve a problem?"

Every Enneagram 5 knows this is an area where they shine. Excited to dive deep into a problem, uncover the root cause, and clear the path to a solution, they are often the people on the team everyone goes to with their inquiries. Multiple examples may jump to their mind when they are asked this question, so the only tricky part may be determining which one is the most appropriate for the role they're interviewing for. If they come prepared with an impactful instance in mind, their answer is sure to blow the interviewer away.

If you're a type 5, slow down as you work through your mental process, and watch your interviewer carefully to not go too far too fast. Allow them to ask you questions; they may be surprised to find you can easily answer them all, no matter how detailed or tactical they may be. Talk about what you've learned and the tools you've used. Don't forget to talk about your interactions with past team members and how you showed up as the MVP of the team by solving their problem.

This may surprise you as a 5, but your excitement and vast knowledge around a subject can make you seem like a know-it-all at times. Family and friends may zone out while you talk at length about your favorite subject. Click with your interviewer while you answer their questions: Look for expressions of interest over obligatory eye contact and give them room to follow up. When giving a past example, be vulnerable by pointing out any small mistakes you made or showing you were open to other approaches from your team members.

Question that may be more difficult to answer:

"Can you give me an example of a time when you had to make an impactful split-second decision?"

My 5 wing is strong enough that this question sends shivers down my spine. I am someone who loves to have as much information as possible when making a big decision, and that's what impactful means: big. If you're interviewing for a mid- to senior-level position, it's imperative your example carries weight. Your decision needs to have strongly influenced your project, your customer, or your relationship with your manager.

Type 5s have amazing judgment and are usually right, but they may be confused as to why this is. They credit their sound conclusions to all their thorough investigation. While research may help them feel more comfortable, I would bet that assessment is incorrect. In many cases, a 5 is going to find information confirming what they already know. Their lack of trust in their gut instincts or their fear of quick decision-making could be a dealbreaker for a team who needs to move quickly.

If you are a 5 and are ever asked this question, move past the discomfort and find an example. I'm sure you can think of a time your manager was frustrated with how long it took you to finish a project and pressured you into deciding how to move forward, and I bet your answer was still correct because you'd already done so much research to back it up. If an example doesn't come to mind right away, don't be afraid to ask for a minute before responding; after all, you want to give the interviewer the best and most concise answer possible.

While it's always great to have a positive story that makes you look like a hero, notice this question does not ask if your decision was successful. In fact, it may be better to share an example where the choice you made was too hasty and created a problem you had to personally resolve and learn from. If anything, this will prove to your interviewer that your research superpower is vital.

An ideal example will demonstrate a good balance between quick decision-making and gathering the information you need to reach an impactful and helpful result for customers and your team.

Subtypes

Let's consider how subtypes can impact your performance in an interview. If you don't know your subtype, consider which of these three options resonates most with your experiences.

Self-preservation 5s may have the hardest time in an interview setting, where the spotlight is on them. It is often challenging for them to express themselves, and they may rely on mirroring the interviewer's body language and mannerisms to feel comfortable. It is harder for them to determine if the role is a right fit, as they may not want to rock the boat by asking big questions. If you're a self-preservation 5, be sure to tell the interviewer if you need a bathroom or water break.

Social 5s may have more energy and information to bring to an interview. They are so interested in collecting facts they often show up as an expert, or they may name-drop authorities they know (or feel like they know through their writing or other work). These 5s should be careful not to project superiority in an interview setting.

The one-to-one Enneagram 5s might be looking for the perfect job or hiring manager. They may feel the need to "test" the interviewer to see if the role is as ideal as they have hoped. They want to feel safe in a job that meets their needs. While they don't want to come off as aggressive during an interview, they should ask questions to determine if it's the right fit, so they can remove their hat from the ring if needed.

If you are a 5, tap into your 4 wing during an interview by talking about the unique qualities you possess other candidates might not. If your interviewer asks about any classes you've taken or any hobbies you have, feel free to geek out about your favorite board games or a carpentry class you're taking (without getting too in the weeds, of course).

The great thing about having a 6 wing is you're good at anticipating setbacks while preparing; just don't let yourself go too far. Flex your worst-case scenario mindset to brainstorm areas you feel weakest in. Plan to address them with the interviewer in a non-defensive way. Use a timer to only allow yourself to prep for a short amount of time—I recommend 20 to 40 minutes max. During the interview, you can use your 6 wing to take a step back and consider the STAR example you're using from a community perspective rather than an individual one. Show the interviewer you can be a team player, even if you typically prefer working alone.

In a stressful interview situation, you may feel yourself shift to 7. Try not to go on a tangent or become scattered in your story. Stick to your STAR talking points to keep yourself on track—and if you're prone to forgetfulness when stressed, don't be afraid to bring a small notepad with a brief outline. After the interview, if you're feeling residual stress, treat yourself: Try out a new restaurant for lunch or take the rest of the day off to allow yourself to come back to equilibrium.

If you're feeling secure in your interview, you may find yourself speaking excitedly, only to be confused at the interviewer's reaction. When you go to 8, you speak passionately, but it can come off as aggressive or argumentative. With my strong 5 wing, it's easy for me to slide into this space, and I have a hard time realizing it until someone stops me or accuses me of thinking I'm smarter than them. Ouch. If you notice yourself becoming excited, pace the speed of your communication and watch your discussion partner more closely for cues of misalignment.

Enneagram 5's orientation to time is the past, and as they're so detail-oriented, they are probably the best at remembering a given situation with scrupulousness. If you're a 5, work on streamlining your STAR responses and including only the pertinent details for the interviewer. It may be helpful to run your answers by a friend or family member when preparing for your interview to get objective feedback. If you find yourself stressed during the interview and moving to 7, your orientation to time switches to the future. Try to use this to translate how your experience will set you up for future success in this role and share with the interviewer the aspects that are most exciting to you. Showing up confidently to the interview might help you feel more in the present moment, moving you into 8. Use this to your advantage by paying closer attention to the interviewer's body language cues and how you're presenting while answering their questions.

As a 5, you may retreat into yourself when you're in an interview setting, and it shows in your body language when you sit back as far as you can in your chair, cross your legs or arms, and avoid eye contact with the interviewer. Pay attention to how you are coming across, and put extra care into leaning forward, smiling, and remaining open with your posture. Some of your typical body language may make it seem like you are less interested in the role or like you think you're "above" it, even though that is the furthest thought from your mind. Body language may be more difficult for you than for some of the other types, so don't be afraid to practice with friends and family members and ask how you can improve.

Questions to Ask the Interviewer

Environment is a serious consideration for an Enneagram 5, as it can impact your energy. You want to ask the interviewer questions they will answer honestly, so you can evaluate your comfort level working in this role day to day.

"Before I accept this role, can I see my potential workspace and meet the team members I will be working with?"

This may be tricky for several reasons—remote work, security concerns, NDAs, etc.— but it will help you get a feel for whether the environment will set you up for success. Being refused a tour even if there are no security concerns could be a red flag.

When you check out the space, you'll want to consider if your desk will be in an open format or in a closed office, how many days you'll be expected to come into the office versus work remotely, how often you'll be in meetings, how much light you'll have in your space, and what time of day coworkers will begin to arrive or leave. When you meet your potential coworkers, take a moment to imagine yourself working with them. How do you imagine it would feel if they came to you in the middle of the workday and asked for your input?

"In this role, is it better to be a subject-matter expert or a jack-of-all-trades?"

You probably prefer being a subject-matter expert, especially if it's an area you are passionate about. This question will help you determine if it is expected or valued at the company or if they prefer to work with folks who do a little bit of everything. This may be specific to the role, and you should already have a good sense from the job description, but sometimes company culture comes into play, so you may be surprised by the response.

"If I think of a question after this interview is over, is it okay for me to reach out to you?"

As a 5, your processing of the interview itself may be delayed, and several questions may flood your brain after it's over. Check with your interviewer to see if they're open to further questions outside of the interview room. This can be a sneaky way to evaluate how you performed in the interview: Chances are if their impressions of you are good, they will be more than willing to keep talking to you. If they are closed off, they may either have fantastic boundaries, a policy prohibiting them from talking to you after the interview, or a lack of interest in you as a candidate.

It can be helpful to practice reading your audience, including their body language and facial expressions, to know if you're on the right track. Look for signs you're going on too long: less focused eye contact, fidgeting, or gentle interruptions. It's perfectly fine to ask, "Is it helpful for me to talk more about X, or would you prefer we change the subject?" You can provide a natural fork in the road: "Would you rather hear more about the research and tools I used, or my interactions with my other team members?" If they say both, they've given you consent to share all those juicy details you love. You're off to the races!

Reflection Questions

1. What values and skills are most salient for the interviewer? This should be clear based on the job description. Find three behavioral interview questions you want to prepare for and come up with STAR examples for each one.
2. What helps you focus on doing your best work? Make a list of any environmental accommodations you need to set yourself up for success, then ask your interviewer about them.
3. What body language clues do your friends and family give you when you start to go off track or ramble? Take note of this for future interviews, where you want to be more concise, so the interviewer doesn't need to wrangle you.

Hiring Managers: Asking the Interview Questions

As I mentioned earlier in this chapter, I love data and detail, so I was thrilled when I saw the hiring manager on the loop had included a novel's worth of transcribed interview notes. Interviewers often don't include enough information, leaving me to fill in the gaps or ask more questions during a debrief, so I relished this rare opportunity.

Several minutes into reading the prose-like notes, however, I realized the hiring manager had only asked one interview question, and it barely touched upon one of the two values they were supposed to evaluate. Skimming quickly, my heart sank: While they had spared no detail, they had focused on a lot of specifics we didn't need. It was clear they had spent time diving deep on consumer behavior trends—

an area they and the candidate both found interesting— but the hiring manager's hopes had been shattered when they found the candidate wasn't as much of an expert as they had wanted. I gave the hiring manager feedback that next time their responsibility was to cover the values required for the role, even if they had to curtail a conversation they were enjoying to gently redirect the candidate.

That wasn't the only problem with this interview loop. This suspected Enneagram 5 hiring manager had talked to the recruiter about how exhausting the whole process was becoming. They couldn't contribute the necessary level of energy to their day-to-day job - they felt the interview process was sucking the life out of them (as an aside, this is one reason why you often find 5s in individual contributor roles).

As a 5, your energy can quickly be drained by taking on too many interviews at a time. You may want to consider delegating the interviews at the beginning of the hiring process to save energy, so you only need to interview people who are pre-vetted and qualified for your role. You may want to limit the number of interviews you do per week. Consider batching your interviews into one day of the week; you know it will take a lot out of you, but this way, you can take more time to treat yourself and recharge afterward.

You will not have trouble gathering a thorough number of facts from your candidates, but you do want to be sure to ask them enough overarching questions. Two or three questions doesn't seem like a lot, but when you geek out on gathering as much detail as possible, you'd be surprised how hard it can feel to switch to the next big question. Become comfortable with collecting enough information from each question without striving for contextual perfection. Asking follow-up questions is a strength of yours, but it can come off as interrogation to some candidates. Wait for them to finish their sentences and ask your questions in a friendly and curious manner.

Depending on how aware you are of your own energetic and physical needs, you may need to go out of your way to remember to ask a candidate if they would like a break to grab something to drink or use the restroom (and if you're in the middle of a marathon of interviews, you may be relieved when they take you up on the offer!). Try to be extra friendly with candidates: Smile, nod, and encourage them as much as possible. You may not have much of a poker face compared to other types, so try not to look disappointed or concerned by their responses, otherwise it may negatively impact your connection. Lean into your curiosity about their experiences and check your unconscious biases as much as possible.

Subtypes

Let's consider how subtypes can impact your performance in an interview. If you don't know your subtype, consider which of these three options resonates most with your experiences.

Self-preservation 5s might resent being dragged away from the work that lights them up to participate in an interview process. If this is you, consider if you need to be on the loop or if someone else could take your place. If the candidate will be reporting directly to you, I do not recommend replacing yourself.

Social 5s might be easily swayed by candidates who have the same interests or look up to the same experts as them. They should make sure they're listening to what the candidate is saying rather than waiting for what they want to hear during the interview.

The one-to-one Enneagram 5s may be excited to connect with someone in this setting and should not "test" the candidate too much. They need to be able to continue the conversation and create a good experience, even if they don't feel like the candidate is meeting the needs for the role.

If you're a 5, tap into your 4 wing whenever you identify with a candidate's experience of being different from their team members, feeling like an outcast in any way, or expressing their vulnerabilities and creative leanings. Show them you value their unique experience, and they can be vulnerable in the interview.

Tap into your 6 wing by playing devil's advocate and asking provocative questions like "What if you had made a different choice?" This is going to get you a hypothetical response, which is not always as helpful, but you can evaluate if the candidate is able to demonstrate flexible thinking and openness to other perspectives. If you task them with a case study in an interview, this skill will come in very handy. Pretend to be a difficult client and enthusiastically ask them all the hard questions you can think of.

If the interview isn't going perfectly, lean into your 7 in stress. Switch to a totally different interview question. Give the candidate more time to ask you questions and see where they lead. Pivot to asking them to work on a problem you're currently trying to solve. Take the pressure off the situation for both of you and find a different strategy. Trust you will have the information you need to be able to make the right decision, even if you mix things up.

When you're feeling confident in your interviewing skills, the power dynamic between you and the candidate will feel very clear: You are the authority in the room, like an 8. Make sure you're not coming off as too intense or assertive with your line of questioning and you're providing some positive responses.

With your orientation to time in the past, you may find yourself thinking of your own experiences like the candidate's. Don't accidentally layer over your own story in your mind or make assumptions about the candidate. Listen to their individual take to come to an objective opinion. If you are in a stressful interview and acting like a 7, don't let your thoughts drift to what you'll be having for lunch or what you're going to tackle next on your to-do list. Keep yourself in the interview by focusing on taking notes. When feeling confident in your interviewing like an 8, you'll find it easiest to stay in the moment with the candidate.

As a woman who has spent much of her career in tech, I absolutely hate giving this feedback, but 5s should ensure they are smiling as much as possible during an interview. This is especially true if the candidate is talking about an industry or topic that bores them. If the interview is not going well, do your best to stay as open and hopeful as possible, and don't forget to show it in your body language: Lean forward and look excited to hear their response.

Interviewing Other Types

If you are in an interview and the candidate is defensive or bristling at the questions you're asking, consider they may also be a 5 and may need you to set a different tone. Tell them something vulnerable about your own experience to show them it's a safe place and you aren't harshly judging their examples. Ask them if they have a different story they want to share to answer your question.

Keep an eye on the clock, but don't make it too obvious to the candidate, as they may think you're bored. It's easy to get sucked into an example and completely lose track of time during an interview. As an interviewer, it's your responsibility to use the time wisely and keep the conversation on track. Keep yourself honest by setting a specific amount of time for each part of the interview. As a general guideline, I like to use five to ten minutes for introductions, 20 minutes for the first overarching question, 20 minutes for the next, and the remaining time for allowing the candidate to ask their own questions.

If you are a 5 looking to diversify your team, consider seeking a 2 or an 8, as both types will push you to bring a more robust version of yourself to the workplace. The 2 will push your emotional comfort zone and help you consider team dynamics or crucial context when working cross-organizationally or with different stakeholders. The 8 will push you to make decisions more quickly and fail fast to get to results. These personality types tend to respect each other and appreciate each other's direct communication.

You may find you have biases against 2s in interview settings, so be as grounded as you can. Notice your reactions if they talk about feelings or team relationship dynamics. Consider them within the context of your current team: Will they get along well with the other personality types? Will they fill a gap and make the group even more cohesive? Can you set boundaries with them if you don't have the energy to meet their need for closeness?

In interviews, 7s may rub you the wrong way, either due to their salesy personality type or they remind you of how you behave when you are stressed. Encourage them to get deeper with you in the interview to adequately determine if they are a fit. They may not feel comfortable getting vulnerable, but you can encourage them to provide more detail by actively demonstrating interest and increasing your energy level. If you aren't getting the depth you need, consider a hands-on pivot to see how they work and how you might work together—they may be the perfect person to bring on board if you're looking for someone to lead blue-sky brainstorming activities!

Reflection Questions

1. Take stock of your energy level before putting an interview in your calendar. Is there a time of day when you have more energy to contribute? Do you work best when dedicating a day to interviews so you don't have to switch context too often? Work with your recruiter to find a process that works for you, as it will result in better interview quality.
2. Have you had any recent interviews where you fell down a rabbit hole with the candidate? It's your responsibility to keep both of you on track. If you find you want to further discuss a topic with a promising candidate, make a note to reach out after they're hired to grab coffee and geek out.
3. What excites you about this role or this candidate? At least one of your questions should intersect with this value to keep your interest in the interview high.

CHAPTER 10

Enneagram 6 – The Loyalist

"I have learned that courage was not the absence of fear, but the triumph over it."

—Maya Angelou

WHEN I WAS young, I didn't know anything about the Enneagram or anxiety. What I did know was the sick, heavy feeling in the pit of my stomach when I was called on in class. I knew how it felt to have a sudden, persistent thought something terrible might happen to me or someone I loved and I wanted to do everything I could to prepare myself for heartache in advance. I knew I had a lot to contribute to my friends, family, and community, but often my contributions were seen as pessimistic, and I had to put more effort into seeming "normal" so my community would still be there in case I ever needed to lean on them.

As I started my career, I realized these were symptoms of anxiety. Stemming from childhood trauma, I felt the world was an unsafe place, and I acted accordingly. This paid off when it came to accomplishment and following the linear path I had set out for myself. I was rewarded by our culture and my community to keep it going;

my actions benefited them. This makes sense: Scientists have found there is often at least one anxious chimpanzee in the troop to keep an eye out for predators and make sure everyone else is safe. On my projects, I was always looking out for potential issues down the road and coming up with contingency plans. If family or close friends ever forgot something or wanted help, I was always a quick phone call away.

There was a cost to all of this: My work-life balance and my mental and physical health. I have spent a lot of time in therapists' offices working on my anxiety, and I'm proud of my efforts to better understand myself and give myself better tools for success, as I know anxiety will be a companion of mine for life.

I discovered the Enneagram during my maternity leave, and when I realized I'm a phobic type 6, it all clicked. There was nothing wrong with me; in fact, Enneagram 6 is thought to be the most common type.

How has this shown up for me in interviews? While I've always had anxiety as a sidekick, I also had supportive parents who believed I could do whatever I wanted to. In high school and college, I took rigorous classes taught by instructors who pushed me, forcing me to find tools to reckon with my anxiety every day. On top of it all, I had big dreams for my career and lots of ideas, so I didn't have time to let my anxiety take control. Sometimes I think of this as "leaning into" a counterphobic approach to my Enneagram 6 personality; I had to be intentional and actively work against adversity.

Even today, I often ask a higher power to grant me the career confidence I had at 20 before the corporate world whipped me into shape, but if I'm honest with myself, I think I had just been powering through fear. In my first interviews, I asserted to my interviewers I could do the job. I took a brute force approach to moving through my anxiety by faking it until I made it, and it worked. I'm sure it was clear to interviewers I was nervous, but I think they saw how much I cared about my performance in the interview and how badly I wanted the role. Trembling through my first internships, following my interests, and leaning into my desire to learn, I built the skills required to grow my career.

Whenever I feel anxious or frozen in fear, I find moving through it is the only way out. Since I can't be there to physically push you into the interview room, let's get into this chapter to discover methods for facing your fears on your own.

Enneagram 6s are great at finding problems. As you're getting ready for an interview, you might question every single tie you put on. You might think about the different mistakes you could make in front of your interviewer. When you go through your STAR examples, the areas of improvement may be more obvious than the achievements you should be proud of. The key is pivoting this into a strength: Present yourself as humble and capable of growth, without putting yourself down or diminishing the interviewer's perception of your aptitude for the role.

To help soothe your nerves and improve your mindset, consider these practices:

1. High Volume. When it comes to strengthening your interviewing muscle, repetition and volume are your best friends. If you're a job-seeker, you already know volume is imperative in the current job market— you're going to have to apply for a lot of roles and go to a handful of interviews before you get your next full-time position. Try applying for roles that are outside of your comfort zone but sound like a fun challenge. If you're a hiring manager or interviewer, volume is in your favor, as you are going to become a better interviewer each time you step into the arena. Ask peers if you can be on

their interview loops to gain more practice; it's a win-win, as you may help take some weight off their shoulders.

2. Worst-Case Scenarios. Trying to plan for every worst-case scenario can easily lead to overpreparation. As with everything else in life, there's only so much control you can exert over an interview. If you absolutely must, schedule ten minutes for yourself during your prep to brainstorm and write down every possible worst-case scenario, then let them all go. Tear them up, throw them away, burn them. Unsurprisingly, even as you write them down, you probably already know exactly what you would do to solve each problem. No matter what comes up, you know the next right step, and you will do your best.

Job-Seekers: Responding to Interview Questions

As I waited for a response from the candidate across the table, my stomach twisted with empathy. Her eyes darted around the room, sweat dotted her brow and upper lip, and she was trying to decide what to say next. I knew what she needed from me was a calming presence, so I did my best to take deep, slow breaths and keep smiling so she knew I didn't mind waiting.

The longer she took, however, the more uncomfortable we both felt. I tried switching to a different question, then asking if she had to use the restroom. It was clear she was stuck in an anxiety spiral. It wasn't dramatic enough to be a panic attack, but she was in analysis paralysis.

I was grateful she was with me during this part of her interview loop. I instantly recognized what she was going through. Her outsides matched how my insides often felt, I could intentionally stop bias from cluttering my judgment. We both still felt the pressure—I needed more information to know whether she would be a good fit for the company. I was able to slowly tease out those details, but it wasn't enough to know for sure if she would be able to execute in the role.

If you can relate, you may be an Enneagram 6 (or at least have anxiety). This is a dramatic example, but if you struggle to this extent, I recommend you talk to a doctor, therapist or other mental health professional who can help you manage your anxiety.

People who have never experienced this may not fully understand how much effort and courage it takes for such a job-seeker just to show up. Conversely, candidates may not understand their anxiety might be holding them back, even if it isn't this severe.

There are so many helpful qualities a 6 can bring to an organization, so let's dive in and empower you to bring those to the forefront. (As there are clear differences between phobic and counterphobic 6s, I've included information specific to each subtype throughout.)

Question that may be easy for a phobic Enneagram 6 to answer:

"Can you tell me about a time when you identified a problem before it impacted your customer?"

This is the real benefit of having a pessimistic voice constantly in the back of your mind. While working on any project, chances are you have foreseen and solved several problems before they even came to light. In fact, this skill may come so easily to you that you don't immediately recognize it. If you are coming up blank, ask a previous coworker for an example. They will probably remind you of a moment when they were incredibly thankful you had thought ahead as it saved time, money, and your company's reputation. You're likely doing this so often that I only have one caveat: The example you provide should be large enough scope for the role you're interviewing for. It should be a scenario that was going to result in lost revenue, customer trust, or functionality (or all of the above!) without your intervention.

Question that may be easy for a counterphobic Enneagram 6 to answer:

"Can you tell me about a time you challenged an existing process or group decision with a successful result?"

Think about a meeting you attended where you watched everyone get on board with a flawed plan. Even worse, where your coworkers listened to a leader who didn't know what they were talking about and went along with their idea. You may have debated whether to bring up your concerns, as there were probably previous times when the group think squashed your voice of reason. Fueled by concerns for the customer or distrust of the authority figure in the room, you decided this was the time to speak up. It's best to use an example where you were able to convince the group to listen to you and change course, though the situations that pop into your mind first may be the ones where you were dismissed and the worst-case scenario you feared came true. Show the interviewer how you convinced the group and, despite your negative voice of dissent, were able to drive change ensuring the team's success.

Question that might be more difficult for a phobic Enneagram 6 to answer:

"What's the biggest professional risk you've taken?"

As one of the most risk-averse types in the Enneagram, this question may give you pause. Take a moment to consider that, once you're far enough along in your career, forces outside of your control have likely pressured you to take a risk you may not have otherwise. This could be switching teams when your organization went through a leadership change or trying a role in a different industry than your college major. If appropriate, your answer can veer into the personal realm of moving to another city for a role you were excited about or starting a side hustle or entrepreneurial venture that pushed you outside of your comfort zone. If you can't think of any relevant examples, it might be time to push yourself to take more risks in your current role. If you avoid risk at all costs, you may be leaving money or personal growth opportunities on the table.

Question that might be more difficult for a counterphobic 6 to answer:

"Have you ever received feedback you didn't agree with?"

Chances are high that a counterphobic 6 has received feedback they didn't agree with from time to time. It's not a lack of feedback that makes this question hard; it's a lack of trust in the authority figures who gave it. The challenge is to choose an example where you didn't originally agree, but in time, you came around and grew from the experience. If it's hard to come up with a good example, look back through your past performance reviews through an objective lens, even if it's a stretch. If you are more junior in your career, feedback from a professor or advisor might be appropriate.

Subtypes

Let's consider how subtypes can impact your performance in an interview. If you don't know your subtype, consider which of these three options resonates most with your experiences.

Self-preservation 6 job-seekers are most concerned with getting a job offer so they know they have a stable future ahead. It may be easiest for this type to fall into anxiety over screwing up an interview. This type will need to push past any doubt about whether they're saying the right things, fine tune their executive presence, and focus on giving the interviewer enough information.

Social 6s see the interviewer as the authority figure and expect them to take the lead throughout an interview. When discussing results of past projects, they may rely on feedback from others (especially those in leadership positions) as metrics to prove success, rather than hard data. They may feel especially anxious before an interview, but once the conversation starts flowing, so will their confidence. If the interviewer doesn't come across as knowledgeable or steady, this 6 may lose interest in the role.

The one-to-one Enneagram 6s are the counterphobic type. They are likely to seem the most confident of all 6s, but this comes from a subconscious place of fear. They may be used to putting themselves in situations where they feel uncomfortable or challenged. If a counterphobic 6 finds they are coming across as too intense in an interview setting, they may be more anxious than they realize.

If you are a 6, tap into your 5 wing by trying to quell pre-interview anxiety with research. Don't overdo it, but looking more deeply into the role, the company, and the interviewers could help you feel more prepared and at peace.

Tap into your 7 wing by focusing on the positive parts of your shared examples. Ride the waves of naturally flowing conversation as much as you can. Make fun plans to reward yourself after the interview—and if necessary, focus on those plans to distract yourself if the interview isn't going well.

As a 6, when you go to stress, you get into Enneagram 3 territory. It can be helpful to focus on achievement, but don't get too caught up in how the interviewer sees you, as that can take you out of the moment.

When feeling secure in your interview, you may come off as agreeable as a 9. If you have counterarguments or dealbreaker questions, it's your job to advocate for yourself, even if you'd rather keep the peace.

Orientation to time for an Enneagram 6 is the present, and you tend to handle a job interview like a tennis match: able to pivot and answer quickly. You've probably already thought about most of the questions coming your way, and you can trust your preparation in the moment. Watch out for any verbal processing, and try to stick to STAR examples further in your past (provided they're the right scope for the role) so you know you've already processed them on your own.

If you find yourself going to 3 in stress, your orientation to time can shift to the future, which is helpful if the interviewer asks you where you see yourself in five years. Be careful not to give overly idealized or hypothetical answers about what you would do in this role if the interviewer asks behavioral interview questions (situations based on past experiences); instead, try to pivot to real achievements. Confidence during an interview is the best of what both 6 and 9 have to offer, as you will naturally stay in the present moment with your interviewer.

How does your body typically show nerves? Sweaty palms, shaky extremities, and difficulty making eye contact are all examples of how anxiety manifests in your body, and they may all show up during a job interview. Plan to counter any natural bodily functions that could lower your confidence. Practice making eye contact in awkward situations, keep a quiet fidget toy in your pocket, and don't skip the deodorant!

Enneagram 6s must be even more careful than other types about making sure to fully answer questions during an interview. It's easy to get swept up in a conversation with the interviewer, only to be disappointed a month into the job when you realize it's not what you expected. This kind of resentment is common for 6s, who tend to be idealistic, so ask about any dealbreakers before you accept an offer.

Questions to Ask the Interviewer

"What formal feedback processes are in place, and how is performance measured?"

This question will help you understand what success looks like for this role. You care about security in your work, so you'll want to know how you will be assessed in the future. This may be especially true if you have previously been placed on a performance improvement plan or been laid off.

"What do you think will be the biggest risks to my success in this role?"

This question is a sneaky way to assess how well you're doing in the interview. If an interviewer is contemplative and detailed in their response, they are likely picturing you in the role, and even if you aren't offered the position, they may provide valuable feedback for your growth. If they dismiss the question or say they aren't sure, they may be disinterested in hiring you.

"When making a decision in this role, is it better to prioritize speed or accuracy?"

You may be especially careful when making decisions, even more so if your 5 wing is strong. That's why you want to know whether your future employer would rather you take risks to get work done quickly or err on the side of caution to ensure precision. If they say both, don't be afraid to ask them to choose one over the other, even if the margin is slim.

A 6 should always be aware of their body language, especially any actions that make them look smaller or too reserved, like crossing arms or legs to not take up too much space. You aren't facing a deadly lion attack. Maintain an "open" presence, as if you are a salesperson showing off a luxury investment—in this case, you. If you find yourself shaking, steady yourself by planting your feet on the ground or clasping your hands under the table. I often find when I'm sitting on the edge of my seat, the need to stay balanced prevents me from shaking.

Enneagram 6s are a great asset to any organization and can often be counted on to keep the most vital tasks and projects on target, even if they aren't glamorous. They're helpful in roles that require risk assessment and compliance. They are sometimes found in supportive roles within organizations with a strict structure, like Government, Education, Healthcare, and Law. Positions to consider include Human Resource Business Partner, Program Manager, Engineer, Quality Assurance, Compliance Officer, Paralegal, and Insurance Underwriter.

Reflection Questions

1. How has your anxiety been a strength in the past? Lean into it for both the interview itself and for your STAR interview examples.
2. How can you reduce anxiety with physical comfort? On the day of an interview, do everything you can to keep yourself feeling safe. Is it a cold day? Keep yourself warm with layers or a hot beverage. Don't skip breakfast; keep your blood sugar up. Ask for a restroom break if you need it.
3. How many job interviews have you completed so far? The more interviews you do, the more confidence you'll gain. Push yourself to do more interviews if you feel you could use the practice, and you'll be a pro in no time.

Hiring Managers: Asking the Interview Questions

Five minutes left in the interview debrief, and our group had not decided. This was the sixth candidate we interviewed this month. We had dismissed the others before them for good reasons, but all debriefs had been contentious, with the hiring manager holding out.

The interviewers were inclined to hire, but the hiring manager, once again, wouldn't budge. This was her right; after all, she was going to be responsible for ensuring the candidate's success. I didn't want to rush her or force her to give in, but it was my job on the loop to figure out the main issues and if we could mitigate them. It was concerning our team had spent so much time interviewing—and potentially creating negative experiences for the candidates we hadn't hired—due to internal conflict.

Outside of the debrief, I asked one of the interviewers, who I knew well from a previous project, what he thought the manager's obstacles might be. Was she too picky? Did she have a bias we hadn't uncovered? Would we ever be done with this interview process? He told me this wasn't uncommon for her, and they didn't mind because she was usually right. No one wanted to hire someone who wouldn't be successful in the role, so they deferred to her, even if they were frustrated by differences in opinion.

In this case, we were able to reach a consensus to hire the candidate by building an onboarding plan that would provide a scaffold. The hiring manager didn't feel like she had enough time to contribute to training and wanted someone who could hit the ground running. This candidate only had one area of contention, and it was an area another team member excelled in. We made this peer a mentor who would be responsible for training the new candidate, and we all breathed a sigh of relief knowing this loop would be over once the candidate accepted the role.

If someone on your interview loop always provides a counter-perspective, they may be an Enneagram 6, actively looking for the red or yellow flags in an interview. The underlying motivation for this pessimism may be to keep themselves, their team members, and their organization safe. As my colleague pointed out, while this can be frustrating, it will likely result in better hires for the team.

Other pitfalls Enneagram 6 may face as an interviewer: When first starting an interview process, they may be just as nervous as the candidates. They can benefit from building confidence through practice or using grounding techniques to stay calm and present. They may fear making mistakes, so if you're a 6, remind yourself you're human and fallibility makes you more relatable and likable.

Depending on their subtype and how they present, a 6 may come across as a little "slow to warm" to a new job-seeker they meet. If this describes you, have coffee with a trusted coworker right before an interview to loosen up a bit and allow warmth to transfer into your introduction.

Subtypes

Let's consider how subtypes can impact your performance in an interview. If you don't know your subtype, consider which of these three options resonates most with your experiences.

Self-preservation 6s tend to exude warmth the most, motivated by building a safe community network around them. They may have the most difficulty trusting their intuition after an interview, resulting in a lot of "on the fence" opinions, especially if they don't know how the other interviewers feel.

If a candidate is extremely self-assured and confident, a social 6 might be easily swayed. They may consider how their manager will feel about the candidate or look for outside validation before making a hiring decision. If a candidate comes off as untrustworthy or provides information conflicting with a social 6's ideals, the social 6 will not be inclined to hire them.

The one-to-one Enneagram 6s (counterphobic) may look down on candidates who come across as too nervous or fearful. Any candidate who exudes an air of superiority will be off-putting. Counterphobic 6s want to come across as impressive in this type of interaction. They should avoid acting too contrarian. If they show displeasure in a candidate's response or challenge a candidate too much, they may end up not getting the information they need.

If you're a 6, lean into your 5 wing by showing your expertise in a topic the candidate is interested in. Just don't go too far down the rabbit hole!

Create a light, friendly atmosphere by leaning into your 7 wing; follow threads that excite and entertain the candidate. You'll get more information out of them in the process.

When you're stressed, you go to 3, which can be helpful if you are trying to come across as an authority figure. You will show you're serious about your work and accomplishments, which could make the candidate excited to show off during the interview to impress you.

If you're feeling confident as an interviewer, you may move to 9, which can help build trust with the candidate. Don't be afraid to ask the tough follow-up questions to get to the heart of their responses.

An Enneagram 6's orientation to time is the present, which is great for bonding with a candidate and following the right threads. If you find yourself going to 3 in stress, you may start thinking about your to-do list for the rest of the week and strategizing how to tackle it rather than paying attention to the candidate. Stay in the conversation as an active listener by engaging your curiosity. Feeling confident in your interviewing skills? Enneagram 9, where you go in growth or health, is grounded in the present, which ensures you're attentive while building connection at the same time.

You might be surprised to find you're nervous going into an interview and worry how the candidate will perceive you. Chances are they're so in their own head, they won't notice you seem nervous—they assume you've done this a million times before. The best thing to do if you're nervous is to fake it until you make it. You are in a position of power and the candidate is looking to you to lead the conversation. If you're shaky or concerned during the interview, focus on your breath and what you can see, smell, and hear around you to stay in the moment.

Interviewing Other Types

If you're interviewing another 6, how you perceive them may depend on your subtypes. If you're both skilled at preparing for the worst, you may bond over being the people your teams rely on to prevent catastrophe. If you're counterphobic and the job-seeker is phobic, you may fall into a bias trap. Try to remain open and listen to the details and data the candidate provides, rather than focusing on their demeanor. Nerves are an indication they care deeply about getting the job.

If you're interviewing a 1, you may find you both enjoy a conversation around creating structure and processes and you share a lot of the same values in the workplace. Make sure they have examples of execution and collaboration if the interview is for an individual contributor role within a team of peers.

You may mistake a 2 for a 6 if you both spend time improving team morale or getting to know your coworkers. The difference is a 2 will look for more approval from others than safety in numbers.

Watch out for bias against 9s, who may have a harder time acting quickly or facing healthy conflict to complete a project. You may benefit from their ability to grease the wheels when you're challenging an idea in a team meeting.

Try not to be put off by type 8s, who come across as more direct than you're used to. Summon your counterphobic 6 side to meet them where they are. At work, they may back you up when you offer a contrary point of view or provide a necessary challenge to refine your argument.

Reflection Questions

1. Are you able to see beyond red flags in a candidate? It's great to be able to identify areas of risk, but don't focus solely on negatives. Flex this skill by asking the candidate more questions if they give you cause for concern, rather than creating uncertainty in a straightforward interview debrief.
2. Feeling nervous about being the interviewer? Ask your peers at work if you can help them with their interview loops to get more practice. Everybody wins!
3. Recall how it felt when you were last interviewed. Did you feel secure? What would have helped foster that feeling? Create feelings of safety to set the candidate up for success, both in the interview and in the role. You may be best suited to help create an effective onboarding plan.

CHAPTER 11

Enneagram 7 – The Enthusiast

"The purpose of life, after all, is to live it, to taste experience to the utmost, to reach out eagerly and without fear for newer and richer experience."

—Eleanor Roosevelt

I FELT ENERGIZED; I had just finished an interview for a designer that went unexpectedly well. We had a lot in common: similar roles, hobbies, and interests. It had been an easy, enjoyable conversation, and I was hoping to grab coffee with her sometime after she began her new job, assuming we offered her the role.

The sun was shining, there was a pep in my step, and I was excited to document my vote before closing my laptop for the evening. Per usual, I went through the detailed transcript of notes I had taken, adding my own commentary about how her examples related to my values.

When I got to the end of my notes, I scrolled down, expecting more. The data was lacking— there was nothing exceptional about this candidate except we had clicked so well. If I removed the charisma, the data showed she might be a good fit, but I was on the fence— which meant no-hire.

Frustrated, I checked in with myself, wondering why I had such a different feeling about the conversation as I walked back to my desk. It wasn't the first time I'd connected so well with a candidate, even if we didn't end up hiring them. I would rather have stayed in the "good vibes" of the interview, in denial, than not hired someone I had enjoyed talking to so much.

Even though I'm an Enneagram 6, I don't consider my 7 wing to be very strong. Yet I felt I was leaning into that wing during the interview, basking in a fun conversation instead of considering the facts in front of me. I was thankful I had my notes to help me make the right decision for both the company and the candidate! At the very least, the good rapport meant a positive interview experience for both of us.

Enneagram 7s are great at creating a welcoming environment and connecting with people over fun topics they're passionate about. They may struggle in the discomfort of a difficult interview, but they can always find something to feel positive about or a way to end on a higher note.

As a 7, while preparing for your next interview, try these activities to soothe your nerves:

1. Get it out. If you have a high-stakes interview ahead of you and feel some anxiety creeping in, set aside a small amount of time to brainstorm everything you're worried about. Once it's out of your head, do an enjoyable activity (or plan one for the future) to give yourself some space.
2. Treat yourself. Interviewing can be draining. If this is the case for you, whether you're a job-seeker or a hiring manager, make a wish list of items you'd like to purchase but that may be slightly out of your comfort zone or budget. Create a goal for yourself to "earn" one of these luxury items—for example, completing five interviews.

Job-Seekers: Responding to Interview Questions

The art director showed us his portfolio of beautifully crafted products and marketing materials from his most recent role at a luxury beauty brand. I was so wowed by his work at one point, I realized my mouth was hanging open. He had led huge artistic projects and worked directly with C-level executives to bring their visions to life. We felt like we had hit the jackpot.

But when we asked him about difficult projects, clients, and organizations, we learned he always managed to exit or switch projects right before things got too tough. He didn't have very many examples of working within the same role or company. He was senior in his career, and he made it clear to us that variety was one of his top values; he did not like to sit in any sort of discomfort.

This art director would have been a great fit for an artist in residence who could follow his passions or a thought leader in a smaller organization that required a jack-of-all-trades. Unfortunately, we wanted someone who could steady a big ship through a rocky storm for a long period of time, and the job was not going to interest him.

While I don't know if this candidate was an Enneagram 7, his kaleidoscopic career trajectory reminded me of other 7s I've worked with. Let's talk about how some of the 7 traits translate to performance in a job interview.

Question that may be easy to answer:

"Can you tell me about a time you had to learn something new to solve a problem?"

This is one of the reasons why I think 7s truly thrive at smaller companies: so many opportunities to take ownership of projects outside of the typical job description. No matter what your previous roles have been, you likely have examples of when a solution was needed and you thought, "Oh, I'll just take a class to learn this skill!" This is especially common with 7s who are just starting their careers, and they are usually rewarded for it. Bonus points if your example (complete with data) leads to your next role or more impactful opportunities for your organization.

Question that may be more difficult to answer:

"Where do you see yourself in five years?"

Personally, I think this is a lazy interview question—and especially tricky in the age of AI, where we truly don't know what jobs will look like five years from now. As of this writing in 2025, The World Economic Forum estimates 39 percent of workers' core skills will change by 2030. That said, this is a question 7s bristle at. While they often love to think ahead to future adventures, those tend to be related to travel or hobbies rather than their career. They are ambitious and always want to keep learning and growing, but having a concrete plan for the next five years can feel more like a trap than a goal.

If you're a 7, I recommend thinking about someone you know who previously held a similar role, someone you admire and "want to be when you grow up." What are they doing now? Could you see yourself doing the same at this organization? If no one comes to mind, what is a typical next career step for someone in this job? Assume you will be promoted at least once. You're not going to be held to this answer by the interviewer, even if you get the job. You can always forge a different path for yourself, so don't feel stuck in the answer you give now.

Subtypes

Let's consider how subtypes can impact your performance in an interview. If you don't know your subtype, consider which of these three options resonates most with your experiences.

Self-preservation 7s often network their way into an interview room and feel comfortable talking about themselves to secure their next great position. They may take it especially hard if they don't get a job offer, as this can trigger feelings of scarcity, but they might find it easier to focus on lining up the next few interviews to bounce back.

Social 7s tend to devote part of their interview to explaining their diverse history of experiences. They should adequately explain their career moves without raising concern they're not as invested in the role as the interviewer would like them to be. If that's you, why do you want this role, and what would make you want to stay in it?

The one-to-one Enneagram 7s may get the most excited about a role, organization, and team they're interviewing for. They should be careful to think about their dealbreakers in advance and to listen carefully to the interviewers' responses without being too swayed. If the role they're applying for has any tedious tasks, they should be able to prove (to the interviewer and to themselves) they're willing to do them, preferably through past examples.

If you are a 7, use your 6 wing when brainstorming potential dealbreakers and consider what could go wrong, either during the interview itself or in the job. Take the time to listen to and validate any anxiety that comes up. Think through how to turn it into a best-case scenario instead.

Channel your 8 wing to come across as not only enthusiastic but powerful. Hold yourself and the interviewer accountable to answer the tough questions that will help you determine if you want the job or not.

If you feel stressed during an interview, particularly if your interviewer is asking about the tactical strategies you use to achieve your blue-sky aspirations, you may shift into Enneagram 1 space. This will help you communicate more concrete plans and steps toward executing your ideals. Try to remain open to differing perspectives while demonstrating you have the skills to move from brainstorm mode to successfully launching a project.

A question about one of your special interests or areas of expertise might send you down a more confident path into Enneagram 5. Show your passionate side, but don't get too lost in the details.

An Enneagram 7's orientation to time is the future, so don't get too far ahead of yourself in an interview by imagining ideal outcomes or scenarios. If the interviewer is asking you behavioral interview questions ("Tell me about a time…"), make sure you are referencing actual examples of what has happened in the past. If you feel stressed, it might be easier to focus on the present, but an inner critic could begin to intrude on your interview. If that happens, name it (in your head, not out loud!) and ask it to step aside so you can complete your interview.

When coming to the interview from a confident perspective, you may find it easiest to bring a lot of substantial detail from the past into your STAR responses. While using this to your advantage, streamline your narrative to stay on track and ensure you fully answer your interviewer's questions.

Try to avoid moving around too much during the interview. You may find this happens more often when you're nervous or excited about the conversation. Take a full breath before answering each question to slow down this impulse. No need to fully tone down your excitement, though; your friendly eye contact and open posture is perfect for an interview setting.

Questions to Ask the Interviewer

"Will there be a variety of side projects beyond the core role if I exceed my goals and expectations?"

The more interesting activities your future job includes, the more you'll want to stick around. The last part of the question is important, as you want to make sure the interviewer knows you're aligned with top priorities. Side projects would simply be a bonus for you if you're already effectively getting the job done.

"What is the escalation path if something goes wrong with my project and I need support?"

You want to know support is available to you when things go sideways. You may be used to providing the silver lining or the solution, but you can't always be that person—you deserve backing, too! This will show the interviewer you want to be proactive; when issues arise, you aren't going to bury your head in the sand.

"What process do you use to prioritize projects?"

Chances are at some point in your career, your priorities were misaligned with your manager's, and it caused conflict. Enneagram 7s want to work on the projects that excite them, but those are often not the ones leadership would like you to complete first. Asking this in an interview is a good way to be on the same page about priorities and have a strategy set from day one. One-on-one meetings with your manager are a great way to check in regularly.

Type 7s are naturally good at coming up with big ideas, being positive, and having fun. Roles and industries you may want to consider include Event Planning and Hospitality, Sales, Product Management, Entertainment, Travel, and Nonprofits.

Reflection Questions

1. What are STAR examples of when you stayed in an uncomfortable or difficult situation rather than finding something new to chase? Your ability to see the silver lining in a tricky position and your capability to execute are what you need to demonstrate to the interviewer to stand out.
2. If your last few interviews haven't gone well, have you demonstrated how serious you are about the role? Have you received any feedback from interviewers and recruiters about their impressions of you? It might be worth conducting mock interviews with your friends or a job interview coach to get some feedback.
3. What have you learned lately? Don't be afraid to talk about recent certifications, classes, or hobbies you've been pursuing, especially if they're related to the job.

Hiring Managers: Asking the Interview Questions

As we walked together to the interview debrief, my design manager was excitedly chatting with me about how she couldn't wait to hire the candidate we were about to discuss. Without taking a breath, she recounted the ways they had been vibing. They had a lot in common, from where they had gone to school to their career trajectories to their shared passion for trying new restaurants on weekends. She already wanted to invite this candidate to the latest Korean-Mexican fusion food truck that had popped up in the area on her first day of work.

She was so excited she put her sparse notes into the system first, but she hadn't had time to look at everyone else's summaries before the meeting.

With no room to interrupt, I smiled and nodded, but I knew she was about to be disappointed. Although the candidate was engaging and eclectic, she didn't raise the bar at the level we wanted to hire her for. We could have hired her at a lower level, but her chances of accepting the offer were slim to none.

As the design manager scanned the notes, she frowned. "Really, you guys?" she said, interrupting our quiet reading time before the debrief. "This is the fourth great candidate you've rejected. I don't get it!"

Eventually, she agreed with everyone else's assessment. I'm not sure if she was an Enneagram 7, but from the way she based most of her hiring decisions on vibes, she seemed like she could be stuck in the same trap. Let's talk about some of the other difficulties 7s might face as hiring managers.

As they love to find the best in a situation and keep a fun conversation going, a 7 may be tempted to avoid issues a candidate doesn't want to talk about. It's natural to feel discomfort during an interview, but I recommend leaning into it, as that is when you'll uncover some of the most interesting and crucial evidence. While you don't want to push the candidate too hard, you do want to ensure they answer your questions as comprehensively as they can.

It's great to have friendly banter with candidates, but seeming too excited about their answers can give them a false sense of security about the interview. A good rapport is helpful for getting more information and building trust; however, if you don't extend an offer, they may feel slighted. Even if you won't see this candidate again, try to restrain your excitement to avoid leading them on. You may accidentally overshare when trying to build trust. Be clear with the recruiter and the rest of the hiring team on what you should and should not discuss with candidates.

It's so easy for you to get swept up in a conversation you're prone to losing track of time and falling short of your interview goals. Respectfully keep an eye on the clock, take adequate notes, and gently guide the candidate as necessary.

Subtypes

Let's consider how subtypes can impact your performance in an interview. If you don't know your subtype, consider which of these three options resonates most with your experiences.

Self-preservation 7s can feel especially frustrated when their interview teams disagree with them on a candidate they like; they may feel as if their team is preventing them from moving forward by staying stuck in a negative place. They should make sure they have a supportive squad they trust to carry them through this process.

Social 7s are less likely to be swayed by only the positives. They are driven to make sure a candidate satisfies the group's greater good. They should be mindful, however, they are not trying to solve everyone's issues with a candidate by overextending themselves in the debrief—for example, by adding more training or onboarding tasks to their own plate.

The one-to-one Enneagram 7s often find interviewing especially fun for the experience of falling in love with each unique job-seeker, with the bonus of being able to listen more easily to the group's perception of an interview. That said, they should be careful to avoid groupthink; if they have data that suggests the candidate is a good fit for the role or deep concerns about the rest of the team's feedback, they should advocate for themselves. If this is you, check in with your notes often and always fall back on objective data.

If you're a 7, take advantage of your 6 wing while preparing for an interview. Rather than improvising or following the candidate's lead, you should come to the table prepared with two or three behavioral interview questions. Get clear on your must-haves and dealbreakers before you start.

Sometimes your friendliness can be misunderstood as a lack of executive presence. Embody your 8 wing to command more respect. Not feeling particularly authoritative? Strike a power pose in the bathroom before the interview.

If you find yourself stressed during an interview, you may become rigid in a way that makes you feel uncomfortable, like a 1. Stay open and allow the conversation to flow, but tune in to the fact that something is not sitting right with you. Rather than closing off if someone gives you an answer you don't like, follow the thread by asking more questions to see if their responses lead somewhere unexpected.

Confidently interviewing as a 7 means you may show up like a 5, with great questions and interest in what the candidate has to say. Don't get too far down a rabbit hole with a candidate, however, no matter how much fun you're having. Make time for your questions so your analytical side can rely on your thorough notes afterward.

Your orientation to time as a 7 is the future, so try not to get too excited about what you could have this candidate work on if they're hired. You don't want to influence the conversation in this direction and give them false hope, but you do want to focus on the candidate's previous experience to assess if they're going to be a good fit. Conversely, if the interview is not going well, you don't want to drift from the conversation and daydream about unrelated things like your exciting dinner date that evening.

Since you go into 1 in stress, you may feel more in the present, but try not to let rigid thinking take over. STAR responses are typically gray, not black and white, so you want to make sure you aren't prematurely judging the candidate. Save your discernment for when you review the interview in detail later. While leaning into 5 when feeling secure about your interview skills, you may be especially good at asking a candidate for specific STAR examples from their experience, rather than hypothetical future scenarios.

Your natural body language is a welcoming presence for candidates, which is a great foundation for collecting information. Try to come across a bit sturdier than you normally would, especially if you're engrossed in the conversation. Root your feet into the ground. Stay friendly, but don't let the candidate know if you're really digging them in the moment— you may accidentally lead them on if your team's notes (or your own) lead to rejection.

Interviewing Other Types

When interviewing another Enneagram 7, you might let the conversation take off and lose track of time. Of course you want to hear about their experiences as a lumberjack in Maine, never mind they're interviewing for an administrative position! Keep the interview on track by referring to your pre-interview notes and the clock.

Enneagram 4s can be very appealing to 7s, since they can come across as the "cool kid" 7s want to impress. Sell the role to them by demonstrating how they can put their unique skills into their work, without getting too excited.

It's easy for 7s and 9s to fall into a groove during an interview when only focusing on the positive aspects of every project. If you have 15 minutes left in the interview and there hasn't been any discussion of challenges or conflict, ask a pointed question about a difficult situation the candidate has faced. You need to be able to assess a candidate's ability to handle conflict appropriately, as that is very difficult to teach.

If a candidate is coming across as too negative or "intense" during an interview, try to avoid judgment and instead focus on the details of the conversation. They may be a 5, a 1, or a 3 who could bring a lot of benefit to a team with great morale but needs a little more manpower when it comes to execution.

Reflection Questions

1. Think of recent interviews you've conducted. Were you relying more on the candidate's professional answers or on vibes? Ground yourself in the skills and values you are assessing.
2. Which values or skills are you covering in your interview? Get clear with your recruiter and the other interviewers on the loop beforehand to stay on track. It may be easiest to always assess the same values.
3. Do you find it challenging to keep a conversation flowing while sticking to the script? Keep an eye on the time and guide the potential hire as required to gather the right information.

CHAPTER 12

Enneagram 8 – The Challenger

"To sin by silence when they should protest makes cowards of men."

—Abraham Lincoln

"I DON'T THINK she could speak up if she needed to in this role," one of the interviewers insisted, leaning back in his chair. He was casually determining the fate of the young woman we had just interviewed for a program manager role.

I took a deep breath, feeling my need for justice rise within me. I was used to men giving this kind of feedback on female candidates, but I had even more reason to be frustrated in this case: The candidate spoke English as a second language, and while she was very well-spoken, the fact that she was of Asian descent added another layer of cultural assumption to the mix.

"Can you give an example from the interview, something she said or did?" I asked, making direct eye contact. I felt more like an Enneagram 8 than a 6 in that moment.

Not used to being challenged, the other interviewer sat a little straighter and looked at his notes. "Well, no. But it was clear, right? She was soft-spoken, and she took too long to answer my questions."

I reminded him English was her second language and it was inappropriate to judge her competence based on that alone. She was a great fit for the job, and many employees in the company were not native English speakers. The rest of the interview loop agreed with me; we did not feel this was a barrier to hiring her.

I don't think the interviewer was a fan of me after our interaction—we were never on the same loop again. While I was proud of myself for advocating for the candidate, I couldn't help but feel a twinge of systemic shame for "rocking the boat." I wished then that I had a little more Enneagram 8 in me.

Enneagram 8s are great champions for themselves, their company, and their customers. In an interview setting, they don't back down from asking the tough questions. They're often aware they can come across as brash or intense. They may not know how to show up in an interview out of fear of intimidating the candidate, especially if they are just starting their career.

To soothe your nerves and improve your mindset, consider these practices:

1. Move. Work out or take a walk before your interview to get rid of any nervous energy. This has both mental and physical health benefits. It grounds your body to show up as a more calming presence for those around you.
2. Be you. You may often receive feedback from others about how you are perceived. You're more sensitive to rejection than other types, so you tend to overcompensate by trying to make yourself smaller in an interview. I urge you not to do this! Your presence and charisma are big assets you can bring to your team, and if you show up as yourself, you'll be more prepared to evaluate if a role/candidate is truly the right fit.

Job-Seekers: Responding to Interview Questions

One of my job-seeking clients was a very powerful woman who had held high-ranking corporate positions. I was surprised when she came to me for help, and even more surprised to hear her confidence had taken a hit.

"People keep telling me I'm too intense or hard to work with, I need to smile more, or even that I frighten new employees. I don't know how to act in an interview setting. I'm convinced I'll make a bad first impression!"

This wasn't only about the impression she was leaving in interviews; it was bleeding into her resume and cover letter. There were several basic keywords featured in the job description she should have included based on her experience but didn't (e.g., C Suite, P&L, global, cross-functional, policy development), and that prevented her from even getting her foot in the door.

She was passionate and lit up the room whenever she was unabashedly herself. While any 8 may receive negative feedback in their career, I find it can hit women the hardest, as this type is the least aligned with how a woman is "supposed to" act in our culture. When she took this criticism to heart, she ended up holding herself back. Having been given this feedback for most of her adult life, she wasn't even aware of how it affected her ability to sell herself when looking for a job. While working with her, I was able to show her how embracing her unique talents and personality (while remaining professional) was a great way to stand out from other applicants.

Let's explore how 8s can best prepare to be their authentic, whole selves in an interview setting.

Question that may be easy to answer:

"Can you tell me about a time you had to influence your team or organization to change course on behalf of a customer?"

I don't want to play favorites, but it's hard to beat an Enneagram 8 when it comes to customer-focused behavioral interview questions, especially if they view their customers as people who truly need their help. Several examples may pop into your mind when this question comes up.

Talk about how you convinced your team to do something different and highlight the collaborative aspect of the solution. You don't want it to sound like you held your team hostage until they acquiesced in your favor. Discuss how you knew this decision would be best for the customer, and use real data, not just your gut instincts (even though those were likely a driving force).

Question that may be more difficult to answer:

"Can you tell me about a process or decision you disagreed with but still followed?"

If you've ever had the same job for more than two years, this has probably happened to you at least once. The key to this question is asking yourself why you didn't agree with a process or decision. Were you simply feeling contrary? Did you dislike your manager? Skip those examples.

Instead, share an example of overcoming your initial bias or knee-jerk reaction. Talk about the steps you took to come to a different conclusion. You probably decided the decision was fair after all or it benefitted a group you wanted to support. Make sure this example has a big enough scope for the role you are applying for and has a measurable impact.

Subtypes

Let's consider how subtypes can impact your performance in an interview. If you don't know your subtype, consider which of these three options resonates most with your experiences.

Self-preservation 8s may struggle the most with interviews as they come across as less polished. However, they know what they want and how to get it, and they can demonstrate their competence well. They should be careful to follow the typical social conventions of an interview, as they're the most likely to make a faux pas.

Social 8s present well in an interview setting, coming across as the least blunt, and it's clear they know how to get things done. They should prepare examples that demonstrate collaboration rather than control over a group project, especially if they are expected to work with peers in the role.

The one-to-one Enneagram 8s can easily captivate an interviewer's attention. They tend to be less enchanted with a role if they feel they need to take the lead in the interview; they want to feel like they are being assessed by someone above their level. They should put their best foot forward while allowing the interviewer to lead the conversation.

If you're an 8, tap into your 7 wing by focusing on positive examples that make the interview feel a bit lighter. Use that skill to dial down your intensity if you feel you may be coming on too strong.

Your 9 wing might help you in the moment if you feel like you're getting a bit too fired up. Try not to rock the boat or challenge the interviewer too much, though a little friction can be good.

Notice if your stress level during an interview makes you want to leave or reject the situation out of a desire for protection, like a 5. Instead, try to think for a moment before you answer the next question, and plug into your analytical side for thorough internal planning. Pausing before jumping into action, especially in an interview, shows you are experienced and mature.

A confident 8 is especially conscientious when answering an interviewer's questions, acting more like a 2; they'll even ask if their response is what the interviewer was looking for. This isn't needy or weak; it shows the interviewer you care and can adapt if needed.

Enneagram 8's orientation to time is the future; check in with yourself throughout the interview to stay as present as you can. It may be tempting to talk about how you see yourself contributing to the company, but you don't have the job yet.

Moving to 5 in stress during the interview may help you focus on past situations with a greater level of detail; just be sure the information you share is relevant and helpful to the interviewer. When feeling confident with your interview skills, your inclination toward 2 will help you feel more present and flexible.

Sometimes your intensity can come off as confrontational, even if you're in a great mood. If you find this happening, actively try to relax your jaw and take a moment before responding. If you are physically larger or otherwise more intimidating than the interviewer, you may want to sit back a little bit more in your chair; just be sure not to look too casual.

Questions to Ask the Interviewer:

"Which responsibilities will I be fully accountable for, and how much autonomy will I have?"

An 8 sees themselves as an authority figure; autonomy is a critical factor for their success. If you're an 8, you may be tempted to take over other people's projects or work outside of your scope; it's helpful to ask about these boundaries early on so as not to step on any toes during your onboarding.

"What are some of the biggest challenges someone in this role might face?"

The answer to this question may either make you feel energized or reveal a gap between your experience and the role that can feel underwhelming. You don't back down from challenges you're excited about.

"What are the next steps in the hiring process?"

This question is a little bit sneaky and is meant to help with your rejection sensitivity by letting you know what to expect. If the interviewer backs away from answering, chances are they don't feel like you're a fit. If they detail the next steps for you, you can remind yourself of that if you don't hear back immediately or if you have a post-interview "hangover" leaving you worried about how you came across.

Reflection Questions

1. Do you understand how others perceive you? Ask your friends, family members, or peers at work for feedback about their first impression of you. You may find there are small body language adjustments you can make to come across as less intense or intimidating to an interviewer.
2. Your passion and intensity are strengths—when used wisely. What's a STAR example that shows off these qualities—e.g., when you tracked down the right solution for your customer or made a big change in your organization?

3. What areas of improvement have you noticed in your professional life? Don't be afraid to share them during an interview. Be your true self; otherwise, how will you know if you're the right fit?

Hiring Managers: Asking the Interview Questions

It was often my job to be the steward of the interview loop: I had to ensure the candidate had a positive experience, the interviewers assessed the right values, and the best decision was made for the company and the candidate. I technically had "veto" power to prevent the wrong hire. This wasn't seen as a flex; in fact, using it often was a red flag as it meant you couldn't convince the loop to agree with your decisions.

There was a loop I was not a part of but that I heard about from one of my mentors. A director was hiring a senior manager to oversee their product managers, and some bright red flags came up during the debrief she wanted to ignore. The candidate had come from a reputable company and had shared good examples of executing the same kinds of projects the role would involve. However, the candidate only had individual contributor experience. Even more concerning, her examples revealed a poor track record when it came to earning her team's trust, and the way she'd presented herself in her interview indicated a serious lack of judgment.

The steward of the interview loop told the director she should not hire this candidate, as it would be painful for all parties involved. The director didn't listen; the candidate was hired. Based on my experiences with her, the director was likely an 8, operating from a place of survival and used to getting what she wanted.

The result was indeed painful for the team and stakeholders the new hire had to work with. It was unfortunate the director couldn't collaborate better with the interview loop; had she sought to understand their reasoning, it would have saved everyone a huge headache.

Let's talk about the challenges 8s face as interviewers, as well as strategies to ensure success. As mentioned above, 8s don't have a problem disagreeing with the interview loop, but they can get stubborn about their opinions. If you're such an 8, I encourage you to focus on the hard data in front of you and ask yourself if you trust the opinions of your peers on the loop (and if not, find people you do trust!). If you're running an interview process solo, it might be helpful to work with a mentor or peer who can be objective and help point out any potential blind spots when you feel strongly about an applicant.

You may find you're quick to challenge a candidate. You come off too direct, or you feel disappointed if they express any vulnerability, which can make them too uncomfortable to give you the information you need. Try to "go with the flow" in these situations and resist the urge to push back.

If the candidate is as rooted in justice as you are, you may find yourself biased toward them. It's a feel-good value to have in common, but check that you're also determining if they can execute in the role.

You may forget to ask a candidate if they need a water or bathroom break, given you typically push down your own bodily needs when you need to complete a task. Be proactive about anticipating needs; if you must, make a note next to your list of interview questions.

Subtypes

Let's consider how subtypes can impact your performance in an interview. If you don't know your subtype, consider which of these three options resonates most with your experiences.

Self-preservation 8s need to pay especially close attention to how they come across in interviews so they don't scare candidates away. While it may not seem fair to have to dial back your personality, it will help balance out the natural power dynamic of the interview. Check yourself if you find you have a stronger opinion than the rest of the interview loop, and surround yourself with people you trust who can call you out whenever you're dominating the loop.

Social 8s are great at selling a role to a candidate and will "protect" them in a debrief if they feel the other interviewers aren't being fair. If you're a social 8, work with your colleagues to address any unfair or unhelpful opinions.

The one-to-one Enneagram 8s may be the most likely to impress or intimidate a candidate, they might need to work harder to make sure they seem open and interested, even if they don't feel the candidate is a good fit.

If you're an 8, lean into your 7 wing by asking the candidate about their hobbies or any other lighter fare, especially if you know you can come off as dominant in a conversation. Actively listen and forge a connection if you have something in common.

Try your best to use your 9 wing when you're in an interview debrief setting. Rather than taking over the conversation and the decision, take the time to listen to all perspectives before you speak. You may change your mind by the time you weigh in.

Enneagram 8s go to 5 in stress, if you find yourself feeling stressed during the interview itself or when preparing your notes, turn to the details. Ask the candidate for more specifics about their project or find more concrete data to help you make up your mind about whether to hire the candidate.

Comfortable Enneagram 8s may go to 2 during interviews. You won't forget to ask the candidate if they need a bathroom break or something to drink, or you'll encourage them if they're struggling in the moment. This can help offset your naturally intimidating demeanor in this setting.

Orientation to time for an 8 is the future, be careful not to fall into the trap of only talking about hypotheticals. You might be tempted to ask about theoretical scenarios, but I would encourage you to stick to behavioral interview questions that focus on what the candidate has done in the past.

If you go into 5 in stress during an interview that isn't going well, focus on the details the candidate provides and take copious notes. Ask more specific follow-up questions to be sure unconscious bias is not driving your reaction when you review your notes afterward. Once you feel confident with your interviewing skills, you may show up more as a 2, able to be in the moment with the candidate and create a good experience for them.

Make an extra effort to have an open posture, smile, and lean forward so the candidate feels comfortable sharing vulnerable details with you during the interview. Release some pressure by telling them up front that the interview is a two-way street: You'll give them time at the end to ask their own questions so they can determine if the job is right for them. Think about asking questions more slowly or kindly than you normally would in an everyday meeting, so the candidate doesn't feel like you're testing or interrogating them.

Interviewing Other Types

Interviewing another 8 could feel like making a strong connection if you're on the same page—or going into a war zone if you're not. If you feel temperatures rising in the interview room, it's your job to ground both of you and create a sense of safety. Having another 8 on your team, when you're aligned, adds momentum to your work. Not being aligned could result in more friction, and in more creativity as you work together to find a common path forward.

In the interview itself, you may be drawn to a 2 candidate, who can help you improve team morale and fill in any existing gaps. They may be able to nurture a team in a way you haven't been able to.

You may be excited by a 5 in an interview, specifically the mental horsepower they can add to your team to support your efforts. If they're an expert in a particular area you're drawn to, you may find the conversation flows easily and you can geek out together.

Watch out for biases you may have against 4s. You may have different ways of presenting as "nonconforming" that might rub each other the wrong way. Lean into your feelings of "not fitting in" or your unique perspectives to find commonalities.

Interviewing a 3 may feel like a competition where you're both whipping out a list of achievements to see whose is longer or more impactful. Their intensity may rival yours, but it comes from outward perception rather than an internal drive for justice, which you may feel is more "correct." Rather than competing, think about how unstoppable your team will be if you're able to combine your strengths!

Reflection Questions

1. Have you ever received feedback that coworkers or candidates fear you? Lean into curiosity to focus on the candidate and come off as less intimidating. Show your interest in their experiences and help them open up to you by not interrogating.
2. Are you listening to your fellow interviewers during the debrief, or are you making up your mind in advance? Harness your curiosity after the interview and remain open to changing your opinion, as appropriate.
3. Can you redirect without cutting someone off? If a candidate is rambling too much or not being direct enough, don't be afraid to gently steer them in the right direction. Too much wandering conversation could lead to incomplete notes or a negative impression of a candidate who's probably just nervous.

CHAPTER 13

Enneagram 9 – The Peacemaker

"Peace means far more than the opposite of war."

—Fred Rogers

I FELT A pit in my stomach before I clicked "submit" to add my notes into our interview software. I had been in several loops recently where I was the odd person out. While hiring managers, recruiters, and interviewers still found my insights helpful and assured me I was adding value, I would be lying if I said my confidence wasn't shaken a bit.

There were a few hires I went along with that probably worked out, but I didn't think they were going to exceed expectations or be successful in the long term. Yet I found it difficult to advocate for my perspective, especially on loops with hiring managers and other interviewers a few levels above me.

As a 6, I do often feel type 9 tendencies come out, primarily conflict avoidance and procrastination, and usually at the same time.

Within our interviewing software, we couldn't see everyone else's feedback until we submitted our own. I had a love/hate relationship with this system, especially as the person leading the debrief. Interviewers would typically wait until the last possible moment to submit their feedback and see if everyone else agreed with them, which means I was often down to the wire in my meeting agenda planning.

Determined to set myself up for success, I submitted this one immediately—after I had spent a few hours completing the rest of my to-do list.

Sure enough, I was the outlier once again, the one "no" against a team of yeses. This case was different, though; I wasn't picky. This candidate had dropped a huge potential red flag in the middle of our conversation, and when I followed their lead, I gathered more evidence proving this wasn't a fluke.

Normally, I would ask each of my colleagues to speak first and take my turn last, but in this meeting, I immediately brought up my concern the candidate would not be able to earn the trust of their colleagues and stakeholders. To my surprise, everyone else on the loop pointed out similar pieces of their conversations that had given them pause, but they hadn't been able to dig deeper.

Afterward, the hiring manager pulled me aside. "Wow, Carolyn! How did you get the candidate to tell you this?! Thank you for speaking up; I'm going to request you for all my loops going forward!" Sticking to my assessment and using my voice had paid off, even if it was challenging at that moment, as it saved the team a bit of heartache in the end.

Enneagram 9s are the kindest people you'll meet in an interview loop. They want to assume the best intentions and avoid challenging interactions, which means they're prone to making the wrong hiring decision or following an interviewer down a faulty path against their better judgment.

As a 9, here's what you can do to prepare for an interview and soothe your nerves, whether you're the interviewer or interviewee:

1. Pros and Cons. Take 15 minutes at the beginning or end of your day to make a pros and cons list for the role you're interviewing for or the candidate you're interviewing. This is a good way to see both sides of the coin and ground yourself in what matters most to you. What are your dealbreakers when deciding on a job offer? What reservations do you have about this candidate that you want to bring up with the group during the debrief? You are in control and you don't always need to roll over to keep the peace.
2. Collect feedback. Ask five coworkers, family members, or friends what they appreciate most about you (or if you'd rather not put yourself out there, dig up your old performance reviews and birthday cards). The point of this is to remind yourself of the value you inherently bring to every room you're in.

Job-Seekers: Responding to Interview Questions

Once, I was interviewing a junior program manager who came across as a yes-person. She was bubbly, alert, and ready to respond to my every question. The problem was she agreed with everything I said, even if it was clear her honest answer would be no.

> "Have you ever worked with Microsoft Project?"
>
> "Yes! We use JIRA to manage our sprints in my current job," she replied.
>
> "That's great, I love JIRA. But this team uses Project. Can you talk more about how you've used Microsoft

Project in the past?" I asked, trying to keep her on track to answer my original question.

"Sure. I briefly tried using it to manage a project, but we ended up switching to JIRA."

"How much experience would you say you have with Microsoft Project?"

"A little bit! I can pick it up again easily."

"Can you tell me how long you used Project?"

"Hmm… Maybe a month?"

She didn't have the amount of experience with Project we were looking for. It was clear she didn't want to say the wrong thing or disappoint me, but directly answering the question would have been more helpful than beating around the bush. A better answer would have been to let me know she hadn't used the software recently but was open to learning. She then could have spent more time talking about her other valuable skills. Most importantly, not being straightforward with me cost her my trust.

Let's dive into all the great qualities Enneagram 9s bring into their interviews, as well as some areas for growth.

Question that may be easy to answer:

"Can you describe your ideal day on the job?"

Self-aware Enneagram 9s understand better than anyone what they need to be successful, and this often shows in the routines they set up for themselves day to day. A 9 candidate may impress their interviewer by sharing details— like exercise, downtime, coffee with a mentor, or timeboxed sessions to catch up on emails— that show care for work-life balance without being too rigid. If this is you, in preparation for your interview, take the time to think about your strengths and what you want to contribute through your work. Consider your dealbreakers, and don't be afraid to call them out in an interview; not only is this refreshing, but it will help you determine if the job is right for you.

Question that may be more difficult to answer:

"Can you tell me about a time you disagreed with a client and had to push them in a different direction?"

It's hard enough to disagree with a team member, but a client? That can be downright painful, yet it's often necessary to get to the best outcome for the customer. Choose an impactful enough example of a truly difficult conversation, when quality, money, or a hard due date was on the line. Bonus points if you had to act quickly or without your boss's approval. If you are having a hard time thinking of an example that fits the bill, make a personal goal to challenge yourself moving forward. Ponder if any of your past projects would have had a better outcome for your customers if you'd had the courage to speak up. Sometimes talking about how you would do things differently can help you overcome what happened in the past.

Subtypes

Let's consider how subtypes can impact your performance in an interview. If you don't know your subtype, consider which of these three options resonates most with your experiences.

Self-preservation 9s may fall into a pattern of making excuses for why roles aren't a good fit, or they may struggle to find the right jobs if their expectations are too rigid. If you get stuck in an interviewing rut, buy yourself a special treat or take some extra alone time to recharge and reward yourself.

Social 9s may have a hard time teasing out their individual contributions to a group project. When working on your STAR examples, focus on the "Action" step— primarily yours. Get specific for the interviewer. Maybe you often use the number of hours you've worked to demonstrate how hard of a worker you are, but can you speak to specifics? In an interview, you're expected to step into the spotlight and show off, even if that makes you uncomfortable.

The one-to-one Enneagram 9s need to make sure they don't become chameleons in their interviews. While it's great to find common interests, agreeing too much with an interviewer or trying to only give them the answers they want comes off as phony, even when you mean well. Consider your accomplishments and what you'll bring to the team. The hiring manager who sees potential in you will want to hire you for all your wonderful qualities, not a yes-person.

If you feel passionate about a topic or project that comes up during your interview, lean into your 8 wing just a little bit. Give the interviewers some insight into what drives you. You can give yourself permission to (kindly and professionally) challenge an interviewer's assumption or stand up for an issue you feel a sense of injustice around.

Tap into your 1 wing to show off any skills you have around documentation, processes, or decision-making. Let it be known that when you have the energy to work, you make sure the work is done right.

You may feel anxious if you are stressed, as you go to 6. Take extra care leading up to the interview to have some "me time" and ground yourself. If intrusive thoughts pop in during the interview itself, try to name the voice you hear and get it to go away. Maybe it's "Worst- Case Scenario Wendy" or your current manager who you're on the outs with, but no matter whose voice it is, it's unproductive. Rather than giving in to it and freezing, use anxiety to drive yourself to do your best during the interview.

When confident, you shine brightly like a 3 during your interviews. It's clear you're interested in the role, and you come prepared with good examples and a solid resume full of achievements. Prior to your interview, try to surround yourself with food, clothes, hobbies, and people who make you feel good and connected to what matters most. This might help boost your confidence and energy going into the big event.

As a 9, your orientation to time is the past. This is helpful when responding to behavioral interview questions, but it may lead to avoiding or stalling on a question if too many examples or negative memories come to mind. The best way to prepare for this is to work on your STAR response matrix beforehand so you know what you want to talk about during the interview.

You may find yourself going to 6 in a stressful interview setting, which you can try to use to your advantage by remaining in the moment. If worst-case scenarios about the interview itself start popping into your mind, do your best to let them go and focus on what is happening now. Use grounding techniques you would typically use in your day-to-day life to reduce anxiety and move into action instead of avoidance.

If you're feeling secure in your interview skills, you may flex to 3, which is helpful when you're asked future- focused questions like "Where do you see yourself in five years?" In this space, it's easy to imagine your future self in the role and show up in the interview accordingly.

Sit up straight in your chair during the interview, not slouching or trying to make yourself look smaller. While it's always okay to think for a moment before answering a question, try to push yourself to answer more quickly and confidently (this is a great skill to practice with a friend).

Questions to Ask the Interviewer:

"Who will support my onboarding, and what initial expectations should I anticipate?"

This question will help you understand how much capacity the company has to support you in onboarding and who you can expect to build a relationship with right away. It will also inform you of the level of effort you're expected to put in as you ramp up— some organizations will allow you to sit back and observe for the first 90 days, while other companies will throw you in front of a fire hose immediately.

"What is your service-level agreement with clients for turnaround time?"

This question shows you care about your customers, and the answer will help you gauge how quickly things move at this organization. You probably won't be a great fit at a company that expects you to work at a breakneck speed. Look for reasonable turnaround times (24 to 72 business hours, depending on the account or project) as an indicator of how well you can maintain work-life balance.

[Ask your biggest dealbreaker question, even if— especially if— it feels scary!]

I didn't provide a script for this one as it will differ from person to person. My question at the large tech company was whether employees were expected to work more than 40 hours a week. My future manager was impressed I had learned from past experiences of working 90 hours a week (I knew I wasn't doing my best work at that pace and wanted to improve). If the interviewer gives a disappointing answer to your question, this is still a good thing: Turning down a job offer is much less painful than discovering a dealbreaker on the job!

9s are empathetic and focused on harmony, industries to consider include Healthcare, Academia or Education, Spirituality, and Nonprofits. Ideal roles include Coach, Teacher, Counselor, Program Coordinator, Office Manager, HR Specialist, and creative positions like Designer or Writer.

Reflection Questions

1. What are your most strongly held beliefs or boundaries? Advocating for these in an interview isn't being pushy or creating conflict; it shows care and passion. Confidence is key; don't be afraid to speak up about a controversial opinion or to challenge an interviewer you disagree with. If nothing else, it will make for a lively interview.
2. What do you know about the role, and what are you only assuming? Check your assumptions to reduce conflict and ask the interviewer dealbreaker questions to figure out if you really want this job.
3. Can you think of recent interviews where you didn't fully step into the spotlight? It may have come from a good place of not wanting to misrepresent yourself, but you don't want to be too humble, either. Show up as a leader.

Hiring Managers: Asking the Interview Questions

The hiring manager spoke up: "You guys are absolutely right; we should just hire this guy." The group started packing up their stuff, excited to end the debrief meeting early.

Surprised, I asked him why he'd caved— I was also not inclined to hire the candidate.

"Everyone else here has great feedback. It seems like he can do the job; I think I was just being too critical," he said with a shrug.

I disagreed. The hiring manager was tasked with evaluating each candidate's ability to earn trust. I consider this the most essential value, as it's something that can't be taught. Yet I'd noticed this candidate had exhibited both red and yellow flags in this area during the interview.

After a thorough conversation, the rest of the team changed their minds. A five-minute meeting and an easy hire would have been nice, but that wouldn't have been fair to the candidate or the company. Dealing with the pain of a bad hire is much worse than taking an extra 25 minutes to make the right choice.

The hiring manager later admitted to trying to avoid another conflict with the interview team. He'd doubted whether his concerns were valid, even when I backed them up. In the end, he was happy we took the time to discuss his concerns further, and he found it valuable to work through the conflict during the debrief. Let's talk about other areas hiring manager 9s will want to work on when improving their interview skills.

During an interview, a 9 may have a hard time pushing candidates to answer a specific question or provide more detail. This can feel like conflict, especially if the candidate is resistant or has a hard time thinking of an example. Don't just back off and change course; you need to know if the candidate truly can't answer the question or if they just need a minute to find relevant information to share. Don't feel bad if the candidate is nervous or uncomfortable. Interviews are stressful for everyone, help them feel at ease.

You may struggle with keeping a candidate on track during an interview. It's okay to gently redirect a candidate if they're spending too much time rambling or dancing around a question. Say something like "This is so interesting, but we only have 15 minutes left. I'd like to hear more about [insert topic you want to redirect them to]."

Subtypes

Self-preservation 9s should check in with themselves and the candidate before beginning the interview to make sure they don't need more coffee, water, or a bathroom break first. If they start out with a plan for what they need to get out of the interview, they will be able to stay on track and make a great impression.

Social 9s are adept at figuring out how well a candidate would fit in with their team or how well they would be able to work together. They conduct interviews well; they like to engage in these types of conversations, and they are better than most other types at giving a candidate the spotlight to share their experiences. They should keep themselves and the candidate honest by not shying away from follow-up questions that may feel "pushy."

The one-to-one Enneagram 9s might accidentally allow candidates to take too much of a lead during a conversation as a way of avoiding conflict or making a good impression. They should trust they are the authority in the room and need to lead.

If you're an Enneagram 9 and you feel you're not coming off as a leader in the interview room, use your 8 wing. Being direct and assertive will lead to the best outcome for the interview while showing the candidate that you are in charge.

Feeling scattered before or during an interview? Use your 1 wing to give yourself the gift of organization ahead of time. Create a hiring matrix to help you "grade" each candidate, and walk yourself through your personal preparation process so you have something to lean on if needed. Search for examples of hiring rubrics or put your requirements into AI if you haven't built one before and be sure to check for bias along the way.

If an interview is on a downward spiral, you may feel yourself shift into Enneagram 6 in stress. Don't let your mind wander into "what ifs"; instead, focus on "what is" in the moment and remember you know what to do to get the conversation back on track. It's okay to take a moment to react if something unexpected happens, so long as you take the lead and redirect.

Once you feel confident interviewing candidates, you may feel yourself adapt into Enneagram 3. This gives you more credibility when you step into a room and shows the candidate you are qualified to be in the interviewer role.

Your orientation to time as a 9 is the past. Listen to a candidate's full response to your question, even if it starts off poorly or reminds you of a similar situation that did not go well. If stressed during the interview, you may find worst-case scenarios popping into your head from 6 ("Oh no, this conversation is derailing. What if I can't get it back on track?"). Focus on what's happening in the present moment, then take control and guide the interview as required. Retaining a little bit of nerves and "6-ness" can be surprisingly helpful for keeping you on track. Your Enneagram 3 tendencies, once you get comfortable interviewing, are helpful for picturing a candidate in the future role, especially when you're reviewing your notes afterward.

When you're feeling relaxed, your body language tells a candidate they're in a safe space with you. Try not to slouch too much or seem too relaxed, as that may give the impression that you aren't interested in the candidate, even if it's not true. Try to sit a little more on the edge of your seat and show interest in everything the candidate has to say.

Interviewing Other Types

Not hearing many examples of interpersonal conflict from the candidate? You may be interviewing another 9. Push both of you into a little discomfort by asking difficult questions about past challenges and conflict, and make sure the answers are the appropriate scale for the role's requirements.

A gift of being a 9 is you will probably harmonize with most candidates you interview. You may be especially drawn to 5s if their special interests align with yours, and you will see the value they bring with their head-down work style and calm demeanor. You can also back each other up when it comes to work-life balance.

You may enjoy talking to an Enneagram 7. As with talking to another 9, you may need to intentionally seek out examples that deal with conflict to get the information you need. A 7 can help promote optimism and improve morale on your team.

If a 3 shows up boastfully in an interview, a 9 may initially feel turned off. Try to look past this and recognize that someone with a lot of accomplishments will bring the same energy to your team.

Extremely nervous interviewees who come off as 6s may be disconcerting to 9s, who may have a hard time creating a boundary so they don't absorb the anxious energy. Focus on your breathing and try to make the candidate feel more at ease by giving them some space to answer questions. You can even tell them interviewers get nervous, too. If a candidate seems stressed, it is likely because they care about how they're being perceived, which means they want to be part of your organization.

Reflection Questions

1. Are you struggling with the stress of being on an interview loop? You are part of this process because your team is looking for your leadership and expertise. Don't be afraid to rock the boat by speaking up and creating some productive conflict.
2. Over your last several interviews, can you pinpoint times when you prioritized the candidate's comfort over your appraisal of them? Don't be afraid to ask them tough questions or confront discomfort to get the information you need.
3. After an interview, are you ever concerned you'll disappoint a candidate by deciding not to hire them? Don't worry about upsetting someone (or your interview loop) if you don't think they're going to be successful; it's a blessing in disguise for them.

PART 3

From Awareness to Action

CONCLUSION

REFLECTING ON OUR strengths, weaknesses, and personality types can shake up our mindset when we're feeling stuck in life. In our society, it's easy to feel like we are cogs in the greater machine of capitalism; the daily slog can make us forget who we are deep inside and how we can bring our true selves to our work every day. When I work with my clients, I often find the most valuable tool I can give them is an outsider's perspective of the unique and impressive qualities they have to offer.

One of my clients was feeling particularly discouraged about her job hunt. She was too in the weeds in her job interview preparation; spending hours trying to come up with the perfect responses, memorizing them, and then getting flustered in the interviews when they didn't go as expected. With each rejection, she doubled down on punishing herself with more effort. Finally, she reached out to me - she wasn't sure what was going wrong.

During one of our first conversations, I recognized her inner critic getting in the way, and I casually asked her if she was into any "personality type tests": Myers-Briggs, the Enneagram, DiSC, etc. She lit up and said she had been diving into the Enneagram; she was reading a book and listening to a couple of podcasts. I asked her about her type, and sure enough, she was a 1. We discussed her recent struggles in the context of the Enneagram, including her inner critic.

With a little bit of distance and normalizing, she was able to give herself more space to show up authentically in her interviews going forward.

After working together for a while, she reflected:

"It helped to remember that some of my Enneagram 1 tendencies may be getting in the way of an interview. I was taking on a lot of personal shame and becoming more rigid each time I walked away without the job. The activities you recommended for 1s and questions to ask the interviewer allowed me to reframe my goals for the interview and focus on evaluating whether the role and organization were a fit for me."

While I can't see your resume or cover letter through this book and give you personalized advice, you can use the guiding principles of the Enneagram and your intrinsic motivations to gain a new perspective and shake up your interview preparation. This framework offers some distance: Rather than critically looking at your interview performance under a microscope or letting your inner critic take the wheel, you can consider how you and your "type peers" behave in certain situations. Thinking about how you engage with interviews and reflecting on this context can remove the shame of feeling like you're struggling more than others in your hiring journey.

For example, maybe you thought you "should" show up as a 3, but you're actually a 5. Rather than proclaiming your achievements, you prefer to do deep work by yourself for hours at a time. Your work is just as valuable as a flashy 3's, and you can demonstrate this in an interview setting while staying true to yourself.

The Enneagram can show us gaps to focus on, but it highlights the special characteristics of each type and the benefits they bring to a team. Like many Enneagram experts say, the best use of the framework is to ultimately integrate all nine points. Ideally, an organization should ensure each type has a seat at the table. None of us are perfect, but the real goal is to better know ourselves, know others, and appreciate what makes us different.

As you reach the end of this book, I hope you're feeling a little lighter than when you started, and that you feel more confident about the next step you're going to take in your hiring journey. Whether you're a job-seeker looking for your next role or a hiring manager seeking the perfect person to complete your team, try to think of your next interview as a fun conversation, a way to get to know someone new.

Here's how I recommend my clients take this information and apply it to their unique lives:

1. Integrate the knowledge: Don't expect to transform your job interview skills after reading your type's chapter once! Take the time to reflect on and journal about the questions at the end of each chapter.
2. Create experiments: Based on your reflections, come up with personal experiments for your next interview. Make small measurable changes, then see what works and what doesn't. Adjust accordingly until you find your flow.
3. Ask for help: Check in with friends, family, or coworkers to see if they notice a difference after you incorporate these new practices. Ask them to practice interviewing with you, if you find role-playing helpful.

If you've enjoyed using the Enneagram as a lens through which to view interviews differently, I encourage you to embark on a deeper self-discovery journey using the Enneagram. It's a powerful tool that is used for way more than what I've included in this book or what can be captured in a meme or an Instagram post. Check out the resources section for more information!

If you're unfamiliar with the other personality type frameworks I've mentioned in this book, I encourage you to check them out as well! They can all be equally helpful for reframing your interview experience. My favorites include StrengthsFinder, DiSC, Myers-Briggs, and Gretchen Rubin's Four Tendencies.

As you walk into your next interview, do me a favor and take the following steps:

1. Take a deep breath and remind yourself of your goal for the interview, besides getting the job or offering a role to a candidate: Be yourself, make a new connection, and learn something new.
2. Consider that every interview is equally about the candidate determining if the job and organization are the right fit for them. Plan to hold space for this within the interview.
3. Be yourself. No matter what your Enneagram type is, you are going to shine.
4. Picture me rooting for you— you've got this!

Looking for more interview coaching and support? Consider working one-on-one with a coach who can personalize a training plan for you, conduct mock interviews, and more. I work with job-seeker and hiring manager clients both in person and over Zoom, as my schedule allows. I love connecting with new clients and organizations— especially when we can geek out over a shared love of the Enneagram! If you think we'd be a good fit, reach out anytime to get on my schedule! Check out my website (http://www.hirepossibilitiesseattle.com/) to contact me.

BIBLIOGRAPHY

Bureau of Labor Statistics. (2024, November 1). The Employment Situation — October 2024. U.S. Department of Labor. https://www.bls.gov/news.release/archives/empsit_11012024.htm

Bureau of Labor Statistics. (2025). The Employment Situation — September 2025 (PDF). U.S. Department of Labor. https://www.bls.gov/news.release/archives/empsit_10032025.pdf

Tuckman, B. W. (1965). Developmental sequence in small groups. Psychological Bulletin, 63(6), 384–399. https://doi.org/10.1037/h0022100

Development Dimensions International. (n.d.). STAR Method for interviewing and feedback. DDI. Retrieved from https://www.ddi.com/solutions/behavioral-interviewing/star-method

World Economic Forum. (2025, January 7). The Future of Jobs Report 2025: 3. Skills outlook. https://www.weforum.org/publications/the-future-of-jobs-report-2025/in-full/3-skills-outlook/ World Economic Forum

Investors.com. (2026, February 16). Inspirational quotes: Wilma Rudolph, Jim Collins and others. https://www.investors.com/news/management/wisdom-to-live-by/inspirational-quotes-wilma-rudolph-jim-collins-and-others/ (Accessed March 2, 2026).

Frank, A. (1995). *The diary of a young girl: The definitive edition* (O. H. Frank & M. Pressler, Eds.; S. Massotty, Trans.). Doubleday. (Original work written 1942–1944)

Newport, C. (2012). *So good they can't ignore you: Why skills trump passion in the quest for work you love.* Grand Central Publishing.

Emerson, R. W. (1841/2003). *Self-reliance and other essays.* Dover Publications. (Original work published 1841)

Sagan, C. (1977). *The dragons of Eden: Speculations on the evolution of human intelligence.* Random House.

Angelou, M. (1969). *I know why the caged bird sings.* Random House.

Roosevelt, E. (1960). *You learn by living: Eleven keys for a more fulfilling life.* Westminster John Knox Press.

Lincoln, A. (1953-1955). *Collected works of Abraham Lincoln* (R. P. Basler, Ed.). Rutgers University Press. (Statement attributed 1860)

Rogers, F. (2003). *The world according to Mister Rogers.* Hyperion.

RESOURCES

Examples of Behavioral Interview Questions

Possibilities are endless when it comes to behavioral interview questions; I encourage you to make up your own, test them out, and decide what works best. For inspiration, here are 10 of my favorite questions I frequently use in interviews that could be used in diverse industries for various roles and levels.

1. Have you ever received feedback you disagreed with?
2. Tell me about your greatest professional achievement.
3. Tell me about a time you had to make a tradeoff between cost, quality and deadline. What did you do? How did you make that decision?
4. Describe a situation where you had to make an impactful decision quickly, without consulting your manager. How did you know it was the right one?
5. Share an example of a time you had to deal with a major customer/stakeholder/team conflict. What did you do?
6. Tell me about a time you had to go along with a manager or client's decision when you strongly disagreed with it.
7. Tell me about a time your workday ended before you were able to complete a critical task. What did you do? What was the impact?
8. Tell me about a time you recognized a potential problem as an opportunity. What did you do?

9. Describe a time when you changed your style to work more efficiently with someone from a different background.
10. Tell me about a time you improved an existing process. How did you know it needed to be improved? Who did you have to work with?

Enneagram Teachers & Podcasts:

For those who would like to dive deeper into the Enneagram, here are my favorite resources! (No affiliate marketing here; these are the resources I first turned to when I discovered the Enneagram.)

Suzanne Stabile – www.suzannestabile.com

Beatrice Chestnut – The Complete Enneagram, The Enneagram Guide to Waking Up, and "The Enneagram Journey" podcast (www.cpenneagram.com).

Abi Robins – "The Conscious Enneagram Podcast," "Conscious Construction Podcast," and The Conscious Enneagram.

Other Personality & Growth Frameworks:

CliftonStrengths (StrengthsFinder) – www.gallup.com/cliftonstrengths. Online assessment identifying your top talents and themes.

Myers–Briggs Type Indicator (MBTI) – www.themyersbriggs.com. A widely used personality framework.

Gretchen Rubin's Four Tendencies – gretchenrubin.com/four-tendencies. A simple framework for understanding how people respond to inner and outer expectations.

DiSC Profile – www.discprofile.com. A workplace-oriented tool that maps behavioral tendencies in four styles: Dominance, Influence, Steadiness, and Conscientiousness.

ABOUT THE AUTHOR

CAROLYN ILLMAN IS the founder of Hire Possibilities, a Seattle-based coaching and consulting practice that helps individuals and organizations transform the way they approach interviewing, hiring, and career growth. A former Senior Program Manager and Bar Raiser at Amazon, Carolyn brings more than fifteen years of experience leading cross-functional programs, refining interview processes, and coaching professionals to show up with clarity and confidence.

Blending her deep understanding of behavioral interview questions with the insight of the Enneagram, Carolyn helps job-seekers uncover what drives their communication patterns and decision-making and helps hiring teams see beyond resumes to identify authentic alignment and potential.

Her work has been featured in workshops, corporate training, and university programs, where she's known for her supportive, practical approach that replaces anxiety with self-awareness and strategy.

When she's not writing or coaching, Carolyn can be found with her family exploring Seattle, working in her garden, or building community through her sister venture, Hire Possibilities Home, which connects homeowners with licensed and bonded tradespeople, many of them women, across the greater Seattle metropolitan area.

THANK YOU FOR READING MY BOOK!

I really appreciate all your feedback,
and I love hearing what you have to say.

I need your input to make the next version of
this book (and my future books) better.

Please take two minutes now to leave a helpful
review on Amazon and/or Goodreads letting
me know what you thought of the book.

Thanks so much!

—Carolyn Illman

Made in the USA
Coppell, TX
19 June 2026

82431195R00115